26

Door
of
Hope

Door of Hope

Louise Long

ABINGDON PRESS

Nashville   New York

ISBN 0-687-11179-X

Library of Congress Catalog Card Number: 70-185545

Scripture quotations noted Moffatt are from *The Bible: A New Translation,*
by James Moffatt; copyright 1935 by Harper & Row.

The lines from Conrad Aiken's "Palimpsest: The Deceitful Portrait,"
copyright 1920, in *Selected Poems,* published in 1961 by Oxford University
Press, are used by permission of the publisher.

MANUFACTURED BY THE PARTHENON PRESS AT
NASHVILLE, TENNESSEE, UNITED STATES OF AMERICA

To Belle

Preface

In my capacity as a mental hospital chaplain I have been
called upon through the years to teach various groups the
intriguing mysteries of human behavior. I have taught young
doctors who were psychiatric residents, psychiatric technicians, social workers, nurses, and psychologists. Most satisfying of all has been teaching seminary students, ministers,
church school leaders, and groups of church laymen. These
were the persons who spoke my language. It was fun to explain the truths of such a complicated science in the familiar
language of theology. And they liked it. They said it sounded
easy when I told it. So I decided to write it down in the hope
that it would be easy reading too. In the following chapters
you will find a conversational style and some entertaining
examples, but you will find a grain of truth also. I have tried
to make clear the counselor's task as he relates in a healing
way to those slightly neurotic and often troubled individuals
who come to him for help. Human nature is a composite of
the present and the past. A vivid picture of the inner life of

man can be found by acknowledging some of the infantile realities we so assiduously deny in our modern culture. Events of the past complicate life in the present without our even knowing it. I have suggested ways in which such complications can be handled most effectively when they crop up in the everyday work of the counselor.

I have deliberately tried not to write a professional book in the sense that I do not want it to be "too deep" for the "ordinary person" to understand. Nor is it a how-to book. It is designed not so much to tell you what to say and how to say it as what to look for and what to refrain from saying. It is not a book about "abnormal" people either, though you may think so at times. Most of the illustrations are taken from the lives of "normal" people like you and me.

I believe that the cure of sick souls can best be done by those who have devoted their lives to the understanding and training of souls, young and old, sick and well. It is the province of the church to nurture the young and comfort the old, to minister to the sick and encourage the strong and healthy to care for the rest. The resources of the church are limitless, its activities are varied. We can call upon any expert in the church family or out of it to act as a consultant in his chosen field at no cost. We have the space and the programs both to cure and to prevent the emotional problems that are the number one destroyer of people and their happiness. We can do it; but time, resources, and will are not enough. It requires specialized training. A beginning may be found here.

I believe that there is no conflict of Truth with Truth. Many people think that there is somehow a vast gulf between the persons who counsel others for the State or for private or nonprofit organizations, and those who do it within the shadow of the church. Such persons, if they are secular, refuse to talk about religious subjects; if they are ecclesiastical they talk of little else. But to the man who sits before them squirming and gnawing his nails it is all the same—he hurts, and, whatever the bias of his counselor, he wants help. Human beings and their anguish are the same the world over. Whether it be Jesus talking to his disciples, a doctor talking to his patient, or a child talking to his playmates, all are one. We learn about people from people. Our reference works surround us—every child, every teen-ager, every grown-up is a textbook all by himself. Jesus used these reference works often. He spoke simple truths which he illustrated from the lives of everyday people. He was so clear that we often fear we understand his meaning all too well, so we try to make his teaching mysterious and obscure its meaning with elaborate "explanations." Our fears get in the way of clear insight and confident faith.

If you can find in the following pages a better understanding of the meaning of Jesus as he taught us how to live together and to cure one another's woes then I will believe that the purpose of this book has been accomplished, and you will have learned how you can "make the dale of Trouble a door of hope" (Hosea 2:15 Moffatt).

Contents

1
Who Shall Deliver Me?

"But do you think we should?" Charlie Stone was saying. "Call it pastoral counseling or psychotherapy, whichever you like; we know what you mean. Isn't that something to be left to the experts? The speaker this morning certainly said so in no uncertain terms."

It was the second afternoon of pastor's school, and the bull sessions were in full swing. Bert had strolled across the pleasant campus and joined one that seemed promising.

"You're right, Charlie," agreed Bill Wiseman. "That is a job for the experts. I refer all my problem parishioners. It made me feel pretty good to hear the learned doctor say we should leave psychotherapy alone."

"Experts!" Mike exploded. "Man, do you know how many experts there are in this country? Not enough to go around,

13

that's certain. And what's my poor confused parishioner, Sam Jones, going to do while I hunt him up an expert? And what's he going to pay that expert with when and if we do find him? Will you just tell me that?"

"Mike's right, Bill," interjected Bert. "You men with big city churches may well talk of referral, but fellows like Mike from the back side of nowhere—excuse me, Mike," he interrupted himself.

Mike grinned. "Be my guest," he said with an expansive gesture.

"Well," ended Bert rather lamely, "they are on the spot."

"*They* are on the spot," exclaimed Stanley Naylor, a tall, gray-haired man in a clerical collar. "I'm at First Church in the downtown area of the largest city in the state, and last week I had to counsel with—" (he counted them off on his fingers).

"One, a little old lady living in one of those small, low-rent apartment houses. She lives alone and always attends church. She is the sweetest looking little old dear you ever saw, but I got a glimpse into her soul for the first time last week, and it gave me the creeps. She told me she is the object of a constant search going on by an enemy spy ring. They aren't ready to 'get' her yet, but they keep daily track of her comings and goings, and even of her thoughts and feelings, by a complicated system of radar in the sidewalks.

"Two, an alcoholic who says he wants to stop drinking. He says he thinks he can make it this time, as he has decided to join A.A., but they told him to contact his minister so he could get the help of the church he used to depend on in his youth. I had never seen him before, but he had seen me on television, and so I'm elected.

"Three, a middle-aged man who asked me to do him the favor of sitting with him for a few hours, to keep him from getting a gun and killing himself. He said it was his wedding anniversary and he had been so depressed ever since his wife had been killed in an automobile accident that he feared he might not make it through that particular evening.

"Four, a couple of young people with five small children. They said they were ready to call it quits, but when they had approached the lawyer, he had suggested that they try to make a go of it for the sake of the children. He suggested that they talk to his minister—me!

"Five, a young girl, a freshman in the local college, a lovely sweet thing (and there are so many like her!) who discovered only after her boyfriend was overseas that she was pregnant. She did not dare ask help from her parents, who would have thrown her out of their home forever, or so she thought.

"And that is just *one week!* Shall I go on? No, I can see I don't need to. You all have the same kinds of people.

"True, in the group there are several who need long term psychotherapy, but, as Mike says, they can't afford it; and *they come to me.* Where am I going to draw the line? How am I going to turn away those I feel I cannot help? What will I do with those I decide to keep? And over all hangs the perennial question: How am I ever going to get my church work done?"

"And if that's not your church work, what is?" cried Mike.

"You can't do psychotherapy with all of them," insisted Bill stubbornly.

"Man," Mike yelled, "you *are* doing it right now. Don't you see? You have no choice. They come to you. They come to all of us. We've got to do something with them, and whatever we do is going to help them or hurt them."

Dr. Naylor spoke again. "Yes, the great imperative of the church is that the note of personal concern which Jesus struck shall not be neglected in our modern streamlined society. We all need that feeling that someone cares. There is no greater need in the church and in the world today than to find that someone who really cares. I believe no one is so well qualified

15

by tradition and popular choice as the minister to do just that; to listen and to care—this is indeed the divine imperative."

"That sounds fine, Dr. Naylor," said Charlie, "but you have a big church with a paid staff of five persons other than yourself. Most of us just plain don't have time. By the time I prepare two sermons a week and three or four 'little talks,' teach a Sunday school class, type and run off the weekly bulletin, attend all the ladies' meetings, raise the budget, meet with the architect about the building program, and take part in community activities, it's Monday morning and time to start all over again. By then my wife is threatening to go home to mama because she and the kids never see me."

There was general laughter, but Bert persisted.

"Is it true that you have to do all those things? Remember Saul who went and 'hid himself among the stuff'? Can it be, Charlie, that you are scheduling all those activities in order to hide yourself from the intimate emotional reactions of your people? And even of your own family?"

"Hold on, Bert," exclaimed Dan. "Isn't that being pretty rough on old Charlie?"

"That's all right, Dan," said Charlie. "I know Bert. He doesn't mean any harm. He's just trying to drive his point home." And then turning to Bert, "No, honestly, I don't think I'm trying to avoid anything. I'm just convinced that we have enough to do without counseling. I think that those people who need it should be referred to the experts."

"And who are the experts?" called a voice from the edge of the growing circle.

Immediately several people spoke at once:

"Psychiatrists" — "psychologists" — "social workers" — "sociologists" — "psychoanalysts" — "doctors."

"You see," exclaimed Mike triumphantly. "We can't even agree on who these experts are!"

"Here's Dr. Graham," said Dr. Naylor. "Doctor, you are

from another state and teach all the time in schools like this. Are such arguments fairly common?"

"There certainly is a great deal of confusion on the subject," he agreed.

"It seems to me," said Jim Ransom, who had not spoken before, "that when a minister relinquishes his right to do counseling, he is cutting the heart right out of his ministry."

"To me it isn't just a right," said Dr. Naylor. "It is not even just an obligation. It is an inevitable necessity. The very core of the gospel is that human compassion which one individual feels for another fellow human being. Without that, our preaching is indeed vain. This is the unique task of the minister which has characterized him from the dawn of history."

"There are a lot of mighty poor ministers then," said Don bitterly.

"You can say that again," agreed Bert, "but there must have been a lot of mighty good counseling done through the years, even by the half-trained, the poorly trained, and the untrained, to keep the public coming back for more as they have through all these centuries."

"Don't you believe that 'a little knowledge is a dangerous thing'?" asked Jim.

"Yes," replied Bert, "but I once heard Rollo May give a good answer to that one. What he said was, 'True, but less knowledge is more dangerous!' "

"There goes the chow bell," said Charlie. "It's hard to believe we have been here all afternoon."

The group broke up, but the discussion continued as such discussions always do among ministers.

As Dr. Graham said, the confusion is widespread. Who should attempt to do counseling? What should be left to the experts? Who are the experts? How does one become an expert? How does one find an expert? These and many questions remain unanswered because as a technique, psychotherapy is a relatively young science, though as a practice it is older than time.

In the dim past of human history danced a strange and terrifying figure. The ancient medicine man with his herbs and his frogs' livers, his incantations and his feathers, drove away the evil spirits that troubled mankind in that bygone day. He was consulted about physical illness and mental illness, since both were brought about by the evil spirits with which he was so well acquainted. He gave advice to the lovelorn, with a well-placed blessing or curse to speed his advice to fruition; he attended the bedside of the dying or presided over the prehistoric equivalent of the delivery table, as occasion demanded. He was consulted about the planting and harvesting of crops, and the gods of storm and star were his familiars. There was no part of life for which his help was not sought.

The medicine man was the most powerful figure in all history. Kings and chieftains came and went, but the medicine man went on forever. His person was inviolate. His territory was taboo. He was more powerful than any government because he was in daily contact with the spirit-rulers of the universe. Even kings trembled before him, for he symbolized the supernatural.

As time went by and civilization became more complicated, the medicine man, like a human amoeba, divided into the now familiar figures of doctor and priest; but for centuries the question remained where the province of one left off and that of the other began. Though each had his own work to do, and though each took his place as a respected public figure in a changing civilization, upon each had fallen the mantle of that ancient maker of magic. Each had about him still an aura of respect and fear, to each was given the task of dealing with birth and death, with love and hate. Each was familiar with storm and fire and with the spirits that gave meaning to all these. The doctor was consulted about spiritual matters, the priest was asked about physical matters. Both were considered experts on politics, social behavior, foreign affairs, and major league baseball!

None of this is surprising when we realize that the witch doctor only yesterday, as historical time goes, slipped off the scene, leaving his duties to be performed in a more modern way by more sophisticated personnel. But the superstitions of antiquity die hard, and even today there is, as we have seen, quite a bit of confusion as to where the domain of priest leaves off and that of doctor begins.

Go into a temple of worship on a Sunday morning, and you are likely to find a black-robed priest, black-robed acolytes, dim lights, and soft music. Go into any modern temple of healing the next day, and what do you find? A white-robed priest, white-robed priestesses, dim lights, and as often as not soft music! Each of these priests will admit to his intimates that there is a certain advantage to be gained from creating an atmosphere, and of holding about his person that aura of taboo which has attended the profession since his predecessor danced beside some primeval river shaking his bones and rattling his seeds.

As late as 1500 B.C. witch doctors were still being pictured in cave drawings in the Pyrenees Mountains. In ancient Babylon the priests were doctors, and in Egypt the doctors were priests. The earliest Greek physicians were called Aesculapians (meaning priest). There are, of course, many practicing witch doctors, even today.

In Bible times, which represent relatively recent history, the Jews endeavored to purge religion of witchcraft, i.e., "Thou shalt not suffer a witch to live." (Exod. 22:18. See also Deut. 18:10, Gal. 5:30, Lev. 19:31, I Sam. 28:3-9.) Yet when King Saul's anxiety became unbearable, when he felt himself cut off from communication with man and God, when he became convinced that he was beyond the help of priest or doctor, he turned to the primitive progenitor of both and took his way to the Witch of En-dor. (I Samuel 28:3 ff.) The scripture does not tell us what feelings he experienced when she asked him what he would do to protect her from King Saul, whose rules against witches and witchcraft had put most of her colleagues out of business!

Centuries later medicine came along with the same attempts at reform. In India in 800 B.C. we find a caste of doctors who were not also priests. In Greece, Hippocrates cast aside all faith in demons and witchcraft and so became the father of medicine. Still medicine did not entirely separate from the church. Jesus did not consider himself either a priest or a doctor, yet he treated both physical and mental ills. The practice of priestly functions by doctors and of medical functions by priests persisted into modern times. In the monasteries of Europe during the Dark Ages, priest and doctor were often one and the same man.

At last came the Renaissance. Bacon was the first to insist on the importance of factual information and to expect proof of whatever one chose to state as fact. Heretofore, science had been largely a perpetuation of assumption, primarily the assumptions of Aristotle, who, among other things, once succinctly defined man as "a two-legged animal without feathers." The dawn of medical science in Europe saw for the first time a clear break between doctor and priest. But just as the break from a parent or parent-figure requires an exaggerated effort, the denial of evil spirits led to the denial of any function of spirit at all. Doctors devoted themselves to the body and the cure of the body's ailments, leaving to the priest the care of any soul his patient might fancy himself to possess. For a few hundred years, then, the division of work remained relatively clear: to the doctor, the body; to the priest, the soul.

Not until the late nineteenth century did the doctor again turn his attention to the soul of man; but do not forget, during all those years the priest was in close touch with man's

spirit, studying it, cultivating it, counseling it. The new interest by medical doctors took the name "psychiatry," literally
"the cure of souls." Sigmund Freud, the most famous of the
early psychiatrists, was a man who, himself, had many problems. His work is sometimes called the watershed of modern
psychiatry because of the fact that he made some startling
discoveries about the human personality and its structure,
particularly the unconscious. We might say they were re-
discoveries, for there is nothing among all the statements
made by Freud (so violently shocking to his mid-Victorian
colleagues) which had not been dealt with in one form or
another in the Bible. The most valuable contribution of
Freud was his explaining in the step-by-step manner of modern science the truths that were as old as Adam. The many
intuitions of the race, the songs, the folk knowledge, the
idioms of the language, the plays and other treasures of litera-
ture, and the great truths understood intuitively by religious
leaders of all time, are merely spelled out in scientific language
by Freud and his followers.

Even though Freud, himself, stated that the field of psycho-
dynamics was not one for medicine, medicine took over,
especially in America, and the feeling grew even among
ministers that the only person who could deal effectively
with the troubled spirit was a man with an M.D. degree. But
many people go first to their minister for several reasons.

The ministers are the last of the altruists. By and large,
their interest is in the person rather than in his ability to pay.
The fact that century after century the common people have
come first to the church is an indication that many of them
found the relief and comfort they sought, and their children
and their children's children have followed in their footsteps.

To the question, "Should a minister do counseling?" comes
a loud and resounding "Yes" from the people. He must; he
has no choice. The church has engaged in the practice of
psychotherapy in one form or another for all of its known

life on earth. In the Roman Catholic faith, the ritual of the confessional has used many of the principles of psychotherapy. The Protestant minister throughout his short history on the human scene has faced a series of persons in trouble across his study desk, on the street, at church, or wherever they happen to find him. Let us not forget the classic case that Jesus counseled beside a well in Samaria. All the principles so carefully articulated in the annals of pastoral counseling are followed in that one.

Many of the persons hospitalized with mental and emotional illness have at one time or another gone to their minister for help with the problems that later became unmanageable. One such was Ralph.

His wife, Rena, said to me, "I can't figure what is the matter with Ralph. He was such a good husband for the first five years we were married. Then he started coming home drunk. Sometimes he would beat me. When he began beating the children I decided something had to be done.

"Ralph was more than willing. He was desperately repentant and depressed after those outbursts. At those times he gladly agreed to go anywhere, do anything. So we went to our preacher, but it didn't do any good. The pastor made us kneel on the floor and pray; and he read verses from the Bible, and Ralph swore he would behave himself forever after. I believed he meant it and I still believe he meant it at the time. We had two heavenly weeks. He walked the straight and narrow, we went to church, and we had family prayers.

"Then one night Ralph came home drunk again, and when he picked up a plank and started after our oldest boy (he's just four), I'd had it up to here." She made a gesture with her hand across her forehead. "So I called the police, and they came out. Of course, Ralph resisted arrest. They beat him up with their pistol butts and hauled him off bleeding.

It was awful! He got pneumonia in jail. I vowed that no matter what happened, I'd never call the law again.

"We stumbled along for awhile. Why, I don't know, but Ralph quit drinking. Only now he has taken up the notion that he contracted a bad case of tuberculosis from the pneumonia he had in jail, though that was 'way last year and the doctor says he's healthy as a man can be now. He gets a report saying there is absolutely not a thing wrong with his lungs; he waits maybe a week, then he hunts up another doctor, tells him the story and gets a whole new series of tests. It's about to break us financially, but I can't tell him that the new test will come back negative just like the last one did. He rolls and tumbles all night worrying about his health. I was about ready to take him up to the city to see a psychiatrist, but my mother said why didn't we try just one more minister, and here I am."

In answer to the question, then, "Should a minister do counseling?" everything says "yes." Insofar as history is concerned, no one has a better right; insofar as the need by the people for such service, no one is in greater demand; insofar as his proximity to the people who need counseling, they are at his door before, during, and after hospitalization, as well as millions of persons who never darken the door of any doctor's office or institution for the mentally ill; he is the last of the altruists—persons can always find a welcome in the minister's study whether they can afford to pay for his services or not.

In addition to the above-named advantages, the minister has a right, indeed an obligation, to call on persons who do not seek him out, and this is an advantage no other profession, except some social workers, can claim. They must wait for the patient to come to them. We can go to the patient, and though no minister in his right mind would knock on a door, walk in, and begin by saying, "Look, brother, you need pastoral counseling and I'm here to give it to you," nonetheless he can make himself available as no one else can.

Perhaps the greatest advantage of all is that the minister has access to the whole family and he has access also to the mechanism of the church, through which he can channel the entire family to the best groups for the greatest good of all. Here, again, we do not recommend wholesale manipulation of one's parishioners even for their own good, but the opportunity is there to use the activities of the church for the purpose of preventing trouble as well as for healing the already existing trouble.

But now comes a question to which the answer may not be quite so resounding.

"*Can* a minister do counseling?" We have established the fact that he should (that he indeed must), that he has the equipment for it, and that the need is great, but all this does not necessarily guarantee that he has the training that will enable him to do a good job.

We find persons in all walks of life, including the ministry, who seem to be endowed, as if by nature, with a listening ear. Now a listening ear is really an attitude of heart. It includes interest without involvement, understanding without identification, and the withholding of judgment without moral laxity. Its possessor cannot be insulted or put on the defensive, and his parishioners are blessed. Such an attitude has been so well described by Paul that I must repeat it here, as translated by Moffatt:

"Love is very patient, very kind. Love knows no jealousy; love makes no parade, gives itself no airs, is never rude, never selfish, never irritated, never resentful; love is never glad when others go wrong. Love is gladdened by goodness, always slow to expose, always eager to believe the best, always hopeful, always patient. Love never disappears."
(I Cor. 13:4-8.)

Although the possessor of all or even some of the above characteristics is a joy to his church and his community, his brother minister, not so fortunately endowed, can be trained to practice the principles that seem to come so naturally to others. Even those who seem to be, by nature, equipped to cope with the deeper problems of the spirit, can profit by training. In fact, one with a natural "flair" for counseling is all the more obligated to become as expert as his particular talents qualify him to be.

"When the Lord said, 'The fields are white unto the harvest, but the laborers are few,'" said Dr. Walter Towner, "I think He meant not so much few in number as few in quality." (See Matt. 9:37.)

We all have an obligation to learn, and we can learn from anyone who is willing to teach. This book may help. I have not attempted to write a how-to book. There are hundreds of those on the market. Emotional problems are brought on by faulty human relationships.

The faulty relationship must be replaced by a healthy relationship to you. Having once learned to relate in a healthy, loving way, your counselee can go on to make other healthy relationships. I am not so foolish as to think that you can learn how to do this from a book. I have attempted to point out, not what to say and how to say it, but what not to say and what to be alert for in the lives of your people. I have tried to help you recognize the value of silence.

If you should greet your wife one morning with the words, "Pack my equipment. I'm either going hunting or fishing today, in the mountains or at the beach. I'll try to get either whales or sea bass if I go to the ocean, either bears or squirrels if I go to the hills," she would probably reply, "When you know where you're going and what you are trying to get, I'll pack your things."

Too often we set out to "do counseling" without the faintest notion of what makes people tick, or how their inner mechanisms are related to the pain that gnaws at their vitals. It is impossible to tell one person how to relate to another just as it is impossible to write a book about how one may counsel another. So I have only attempted to point out some of the game you may find in the jungles of the human spirit and to suggest some of the equipment it would be advisable to carry with you on your journey.

As I write these words, I can hear the surf crashing on the rocks outside my window, for I am on the far northern coast of California. I got here by following a road map provided by my auto club. It was a good map, and I had no trouble in finding my way. But no auto club would be so foolish as to print a set of directions with a map that aimed to tell each driver exactly how to handle his own vehicle. No one would try to anticipate in detail every set of circumstances that might conceivably confront every single driver. On the highway there are Jeeps and Cadillacs, convertibles and Model T's, Volkswagens and lumber trucks. Each must be driven at its own pace, braked in its own way, each must be allowed a different amount of space for negotiating a turn or passing another motorist, each must climb the hills in the gear best suited to its purpose. Yet, all can follow the same road map and arrive at the same destination.

So it is with counseling. There are glaring errors every counselor must avoid, of course, but each must handle his own counselee in his own way within the framework of the counselor's ability to help him and the counselee's willingness to tolerate help. So this book is something like a road map of the human spirit. It will not attempt to tell you how to negotiate every turn, but it will warn you that a curve may be imminent. It will tell you not what to say but what to look for. It will show you ways in which the person you have chosen to help is similar to all the other persons you know and will indicate what can make him different from all others in the world.

In order to help a person you must know what is wrong with him. In order to find out what is wrong you must know where to look, and you must know what takes place in the development of the average individual.

"Why?" you say. "Don't the same things happen to us all; we are born, we grow up, we mature, we marry, we produce children, we grow old, and we die."

Yes, we do those things, but there are many variations, many deviations, and many frustrations. The details must be spelled out, and many emotions experienced in relationship to each event. In the succeeding chapters, I will outline for you the development of the average child and his emotional life, with hints of how things may go wrong later in the life of the adult as a result of these childhood experiences. I will try to show how all his experiences go into that great unconscious reservoir upon which he calls in time of need, and which either helps or hinders him as he attempts to deal with the problems that confront him in his later life.

I will try to show you that it is emotions rather than mere events we are dealing with. The events are important springboards for emotion, but sometimes we find persons whose emotions are not available to them on call. Our forefathers were not so fearful of feeling as we seem to be. Half a century ago Billy Sunday had church members screaming and fainting in the aisles; a few years further back John Wesley spoke so forcefully that the tears cut furrows in the coal dust that covered the faces of the miners in the north of England. These men did not hesitate to rouse emotion in the hearts of their hearers. It took a certain amount of courage to handle the feeling thus roused, but there was always the sturdy old altar rail, or at least a pulpit for protection. In a pinch other members of the congregation could be called upon to handle the overenthusiastic or the overemotional. It might take a somewhat greater amount of courage to handle the emotions brought out by the counseling process. You are not in a protected situation. You are alone in the office in a one-to-one relationship, and you are on your own.

We may learn before we are through that we have not so much to fear from the emotions of our parishioners as from our own feelings within. Bert, in the discussion at the beginning of the chapter, was right when he asked, "Are you really busy or are you scheduling activities in order to hide yourself from the intimate emotional reactions of your people? Of your own family?"

He might well have added, "Of your own soul?"

Read the road map. It may help you to help your parishioners. It may even help you to help yourself!

2
Nothing Is Hid that Shall Not Be Revealed

Late in the afternoon the phone rang. When I answered, a familiar voice said, "It's about my wife, Julia."

The man who spoke was Arnie Smathers, an ex-patient of the mental hospital where I was then chaplain. Arnie had been an alcoholic but had been in treatment for some time, and I had heard from his doctor that he was doing quite well.

"She is—I don't know what she is, of course, but while I was out at your place, I learned enough to know she's *something*. I've tried to get her to my doctor, but she says that all psychiatrists are atheists and that her whole trouble is she has lost her faith in God. I asked her if she would talk to you, and she has consented to see you at least once. Will you please try to help her?"

I said I would talk to her, and Julia herself came to the phone.

"It's not that I can actually see the devil," she assured me, "but I am so sure he is there in the corner grinning at me that I might as *well* be seeing him."

I made an appointment for her to come to my office the next day, and she arrived on time. Julia was a tiny little woman with dark, neatly arranged hair and bright brown eyes. Outwardly she appeared to be in complete control of the situation and told a plausible story.

"It all started a couple of weeks ago," she began. "I went out to dinner with my husband, and we met a friend of his. The friend was an atheist-scientist." (Julia always called him "the atheist-scientist." So far as I could determine, she never knew his name.) "He spent most of the evening trying to convince me that there is not and cannot be any such thing as a god. At first I resisted the idea, but in the end he convinced me. That's all. He just convinced me. But ever since, I have been miserable and felt that the devil was after me. As I said on the phone last night, it isn't that I see the devil. I don't see him yet, but I am sure I may see him at any moment.

"I have been very upset by this experience. My faith seems to be gone forever. I have quit going to church, I have given up my Sunday school class, and I have resigned as president of the Woman's Society. The whole thing makes me feel terrible. Do you think anyone as bad as I can ever be restored to faith in God? Can you do anything to help me?"

"I will certainly try," I assured her. "Can you tell me more about it?"

"I have told you everything. The atheist-scientist just explained very scientifically that there is no God, and I believed him. There isn't any more to tell. What I want you to do is help me get back my faith. What shall I do? Pray? Will you pray for me that I get my faith back?"

Nothing Is Hid that Shall Not Be Revealed

We hear these words, "I have told you everything," so often! Julia was doing something that they all do, each in his own way. She was testing me. Would I do what she demanded? I heard between the lines what Julia really meant by what she had just said.

"How smart are you anyway? Do you take what I say at face value? Or do you know it is a front? Are you going to fall into the trap I am setting for you and do what I say? Can you be bullied into using the tools of your trade on demand? Are you going to fulfill every neurotic request of mine?

"Or are you going to remain in control of this therapy yourself? Am I safe in your hands? Do you realize that I am suffering untold torture from many things, the least of which is my lost faith? Can I trust you? Are you worthy of my confidence? Do we continue together? Or do I go home and tell my husband that the therapist he picked for me was a washout?"

I said, "Should you pray to a God who, for now, has ceased to exist? You have lost your faith. To whom should you pray?"

The words I spoke *seemed* to take her at face value, but what I was really saying in answer to her unspoken queries was this:

"Julia, I know that every word you say is just as phony as can be. It would make no sense to pray to a God whose very existence you deny, and you know it. You just want to see if I catch the point. You are also ordering me to pray in order to see if I am afraid not to do what is expected and demanded of me as a minister, but, Julia, you're wrong. I know how you suffer, and I am in it with you all the way. I'm not fooled by the loss of faith talk. I know you have a great deal to tell me that can be cut off right here if I jump down on my knees at your suggestion."

She became rather angry for a moment, but then she re-

laxed and settled back into her chair and I knew we had
made it over the first hurdle.

She then began a long and complicated explanation of her
theology which lasted the rest of the hour. Finally, I asked
her if she would like to come back and tell me more about it
later in the week. It is a wise procedure to set certain time
limits to each interview. The average is forty-five minutes.
Sometimes the person needs a little more, sometimes a little
less, but from long experience we know that emotionally
charged material cannot safely be expressed for much longer
than an hour at a time without damage to the counselee.

No one is going to pour out his soul before he knows how
he will be received. He is first—and, I think, quite wisely—
going to test the person he has chosen to confide in, as Julia
tested me. He is going to confess a few minor sins to see how
we respond. If the reaction is satisfactory, that is, if we do not
react with condemnation, alarm, or a stream of advice, he
will let us a step further into the painful recesses of his
tortured heart. But he will only do this bit by bit, and step
by step.

So I made another appointment for Julia.

When she returned the next time, and throughout a long
summer, she talked about this lost "faith" of hers. It was a
pitiful hodgepodge. I listened through the dank shades and
murky flames of Milton's *Paradise Lost,* of which she spoke
as if every word were gospel. She knew all its lurid horror,
none of its beauty. We traveled the road of General
William Booth, with all its hellfire and damnation—none
of its joy, none of its singing. Primarily, it seemed as if her
faith had been derived from James Whitcomb Riley: "The
gobble-uns'll git *you* ef you don't watch out."

At times I would attempt to explain that the cosmos of the
spiritual world was not exactly as she had been led to believe.
She would become very angry at such statements and tell me
I had no religion and she wondered how I ever got a job

purveying it. I would subside, and she would return to her theme.

These outbursts of hers, and my response, seemed to give her a certain sense of relief. It is always good to encourage an expression of feeling in the persons we help in this way. They can say things to us if they trust us that they would not have the courage to say to anyone else in the whole world.

Every time Julia gave me an opening, I tried to lure her back to talk of something more practical, less "theological." I was fairly sure by now that the theology was only serving as a front to cover something of which she was not in the least aware. She talked about theology all summer, but gradually I began to get glimpses of her real life. I always tried to keep her talking about these events, while she always gravitated back to the subject of her lost faith. After five months, I had gathered a few bits and pieces together.

She was the ninth of eleven children, neither more petted nor more rejected than the others. Her parents were of the old school that believes in handling children like dogs or cattle. They were strict and rigid in their demands on the family and no less strict and rigid themselves. Julia never remembers seeing her father and mother show any affection to each other except once. This she probably remembers because of the fact that her mother sat on her father's lap and the chair broke down, dumping them both on the floor.

With less restraint they fought. The mother was a domineering woman, telling the father in front of anyone who would listen that she was a better business manager than he was, and they would have been bankrupt long ago if it had not been for her excellent business management. This the father never disputed except on those rare occasions when he became angry.

Julia's mother was just as convinced of her sterling worth as a mother as she was of her merits as a businesswoman.

33

To Julia, it seemed that her mother was never wrong, that even when she *was* wrong she would never admit it.

Julia remembers the toilet training that was a nightmare to every child in the house. If a child had an "accident," her mother would rub his nose in the feces, saying that that was the way to train a dog and what was good for the dogs must be good for the children. At first, Julia did not criticize her mother's behavior. Instead, she said with some logic, "I suppose eighteen years of washing diapers becomes monotonous."

The severity of her mother found a pale echo in Julia's father, but somehow Julia found him more companionable. She remembers that he used to take her on the tractor in the spring days and give her some of the warmth and affection she so badly needed. Then her sister was born, and it seemed to Julia that her father transferred all his love to this new-comer. All her life she secretly hated her sister who seemed to be in some strange way connected with her mother. She sympathized with her father in his increasingly frequent quarrels with her mother, though she never dared to voice her feelings aloud.

She went away to college, but had returned to accept a position as secretary in the local bottling plant when she met Arnie. She was aware that he had a little too much to drink at times and at first refused to date him, but he persisted and she began going out with him.

Then her father died suddenly, and the bottom dropped out of her world. None of her friends came to the rescue as did Arnie. He was at the house morning, noon, and night during their time of grief. He helped with the funeral ar-rangements and took especially tender care of Julia. During all the days preceding, during, and after the funeral, Arnie was sober, thoughtful, and loving. She began to date him regularly. One day, two weeks after her father's death, they were having lunch with some employees from the bottling works when one of the girls said, "Why don't you two get married?"

"Yes, why not?" said another. "We need a wedding in this outfit."

"Come on, liven the place up."

Amid the laughter and teasing, Arnie slid over closer and whispered in her ear, "Why not, Julia? You know I love you. Let's get married today. Right now."

She heard herself saying, "All right, Arnie, I'll marry you."

Gaily they trooped over to the courthouse, procured a license, and found a justice of the peace. Julia returned to work after lunch a married woman. She told me of the sinking feeling she had in the pit of her stomach an hour later after the excitement had died down; of her dismay at the thought of living with Arnie; and at the same time of her secret delight at the thought that never ever would she again spend the night under the same roof with her mother.

Not many days went by before she discovered that Arnie was not a man with a little drinking problem as she had thought. He was a full-blown alcoholic. In the morning before going to work he wanted a drink more than he wanted breakfast. For lunch he came home and headed straight for the bottle. At night he was out cold by nine o'clock. Julia's life was worse than it had been before!

"I had never been very interested in religion," she told me, "but I had to turn somewhere for help. I did not believe in divorce. My mother would have disowned me if I had even suggested such a thing, and I would have had to depend on her for help. There was no way to get rid of Arnie. I didn't exactly want to kill him myself, but I had heard that God answers prayer.

"I decided that if I became a Christian, went to church every Sunday, and prayed a lot, God would reward me by taking this man off my hands. So I started going to church.

The people welcomed me with open arms; they gave me the love I had missed from my parents and was now missing from my husband. So I worked in the Sunday school and in the Women's Society, and at home I prayed all the time.

"Sometimes I would sit for hours at the piano, playing and singing hymns. I would feel the presence of God so strongly at those times that it seemed he was sitting on the piano bench beside me kissing me. Then I would get guilty feelings because I had sexy thoughts toward God.

"The more I prayed, the worse my husband got. He quit drinking at home. Instead he would go out to the local bars and stay till all hours. Then I would kneel on the floor and pray without ceasing as it tells us to in the Bible. When the phone rang, I would think, 'This is it!'

"I believed that Arnie would surely drive in front of a freight train or stagger out in front of a big truck in his drunken stupor. I could picture it all: the flashing lights of the police cars; the grief-stricken widow being led away, in a state of collapse, from the identification of her husband; the dimly lit church; the mounds of flowers; the organ music.

"Sometimes I would be so deeply affected that I would even cry. It was strange, but on those nights, I sometimes fell so fast asleep that I did not awake when Arnie came home, for he *always* came home big as life and twice as drunk.

"One day his boss called me while Arnie was at work.

" 'Will you sign papers for Arnie to be committed to the State Hospital?' he asked kindly. 'You must realize something has got to be done. He is a valuable employee, and I don't want to fire him. He really needs treatment. Will you co-operate?'

"Would I cooperate? I was delighted! God was answering my prayers just as all the evangelists had told me he would, not on my own terms, but on his. The State Hospital was a solution I had never thought of. Yet, here was God, dear, dear God, bringing me Arnie's boss with a solution to Arnie's problem (but really to my problem) in a way that saved me all the anguish of another funeral, and at the same time was just as permanent as death. He was saving me the necessity of even having to consider another marriage. We could have a long life together, God and I, without any outside interference. How little I knew!

"I had no sooner gotten Arnie into the hospital than the Social Service Department was calling me in, talking about leave plans. It seems that the good old days when one 'put away' a loved one in such an institution, and mourned him for dead, were gone forever. Before three months had gone by, Arnie came out a new man, at least that's what he says. He was referred for treatment to a student psychoanalyst, and Arnie is enthusiastic about what he thinks will be done for him. The doctor's name is Benton. Do you know him?"

Julia paused.

"Yes, I know him," I said. "He's a good man."

"He's so good that Arnie has never taken a drink from that day to this," said Julia bitterly. "Arnie has his old job back, and his boss says he's a better employee than ever before, but do you see what I'm trying to tell you? Do you know what hell I've been through since it came to me?

"I was praying for God to commit a murder I didn't have the guts to commit for myself!"

She gagged and shuddered.

"I was so angry at God for returning Arnie to a life of usefulness as a self-respecting human being that I quit the church and turned my back on life.

"I 'lost faith in God,'" she said with bitter sarcasm. "Don't you see? Though I didn't realize it, I was praying that God would kill my husband, and when instead he led him to a good psychoanalyst and the analyst cured him, I lost faith in God."

Julia burst into uncontrolled sobbing. I sat very still and

waited for her to recover her equilibrium in her own time. At last she did.

"Do you know?" she said as she left the office. "I feel better. How can you confess to feelings of wanting to murder your husband and commit incest with God and feel *better?*"

I smiled. "It is *because* you confessed it that you feel better," I explained.

We often find this sense of wonderment in counselees who have broken through the barrier that hides their unknown wishes from themselves, have seen themselves in all their ugliness, yet have felt better for it. Sometimes we, too, feel a share of the wonder that we have had a part in this miracle, and seeing their faces shine with a beauty never before suspected we realize fully our own partnership with God.

That same night, when she got home, Julia asked Arnie, "Did you ever wish you could get rid of me? Did you ever think of killing me and wish you had the nerve?"

His response was instantaneous: "Yes, many times."

They both laughed with visible relief, and their relationship to each other improved from that moment. So also did Julia's relationship to God. Because she realized why she had lost faith in him, she had a basis for a deeper, more satisfying faith.

This is not the whole story of Julia and Arnie. It is, however, the part that best serves to illustrate the point that opening statements made by a counselee on the first visit may mean anything other than what he says it does. Whatever we *say*, our difficulties are rooted in close family ties and faulty human relationships. There is always—not just sometimes, and not just often—but *always* more to the person's story than meets the eye.

In Julia's case, it was impossible for her to admit to herself that she had murderous thoughts toward her husband, so she rejected the idea even before it came up into her consciousness. She found it much easier to tell a story of how she had lost her faith in God, and how she felt that the devil was after her. These are matters with which one may approach a minister. One would hardly just walk in and begin by saying, "I want to murder my husband." Such confessions come only after the person has learned to have confidence in the counselor. Never rush the process. Expect to hear more, but meanwhile listen to all the philosophical or theological material he wants to tell you. Eventually, if you listen in a manner that inspires trust, you will hear a more concrete reason for his distress.

The counselee himself often has no idea of what is underlying his statements, or even that anything is. Jim, one of my students, had spent a good deal of time talking about himself and his relationship to his widowed mother. Finally, he said, "Well, you have helped me a lot. Thank you. I do not think I will need to see you again as the semester is drawing to a close, and we will both be busy. Besides, I think I know all there is to know about myself now."

And, immediately, with no apparent connection, he began talking about Dr. Norris, one of the lecturers at the hospital.

"I cannot bear that man," he said. "He is arrogant and pompous. He always talks down to the students; he is unpardonably rude to patients. One of the nurses told me the other day he cannot even handle his own finances. As much as he makes, he is almost on the verge of bankruptcy."

He paused. I remained silent, and after a bit he continued, "That is an unpardonable thing in a man of his professional standing. Anyone can manage money better than that. Why, I have never had very much, but even in school I have always paid my bills. My own mother, who did not think too highly of my talents in some areas, used to say, 'Jim, you are very good in financial matters. You are better than most businessmen. I have told Norris many times he would do well to respect your judgment in financial matters.'"

"Norris?" I inquired innocently.

"Yes," replied Jim with naïve candor, "Norris. That was my father's given name."

A little belligerently, he added, "Why are you smiling?"

"Why," I replied blandly, "at the similarity of the names. Your father has exactly the same name as the doctor you have just been castigating. I was wondering if there could be any connection."

"Of course not!" he yelled at me. Then he blushed and hung his head.

Slowly he began to talk of his father. He told how angry his father had been when Jim had first disclosed the fact that he intended to enter the ministry. He told of insults he had been forced to swallow from as far back as he could remember. He told of seeing his father slap his mother, and wishing in his childish heart that he were big enough to slap his father just as hard as his mother had been slapped. Memories from early childhood brought angry tears to his eyes. At last he breathed with a sort of awe, "I guess I will want to see you again after all. There is no telling how much more *is* there, is there?"

No, there is no telling and there is no knowing, unless we wait with patience for the revelations of human personality that will be made to us if we have the time to listen to these persons who come to us for help. There is no end to the amazing discoveries that can be made about human nature, or about any one individual.

In the foothills of the Sierra Nevada Range in northern California, there is an opening in the earth called the Moaning Cave. In prehistoric times many aborigines took refuge from the elements or the wild life that roamed the country in what appeared to them to be a shallow hole in the ground. Others stepped too far into the shadows at the back of the cave and were never seen or heard from again.

How do we know this? Because thousands of years later,

during the gold rush, a prospector discovered the first of the big "rooms" seventy-five feet below the then-known floor of the cave, and on the floor of the room, the bones of prehistoric men mingled with the bones of extinct beasts.

A good deal of spelunking has been done since then, and each room of the cave seems larger than the last. Some are so large that bottom has never been touched yet. The labyrinthine caverns seem to honeycomb the range near Columbia. An opening that has not been discovered is known to exist about two miles away in another mountain. This we know because fresh air blows always through the cave, *not* from the known opening, but from *within the cavern's depths!* And as it blows, it makes an eerie, moaning sound from which comes the name, the Moaning Cave. When fully explored, the Moaning Cave may prove to be more beautiful and larger than either the Carlsbad Caverns or Mammoth Cave.

Like this cave is the human personality. So little we know of any counselee when he first comes to us! He may seem shallow and dull—an individual with a strange, inexplicable moaning, a symptom of his misery. But no one is really shallow and dull. If he seems to be, it is only that he is afraid to show his real personality. But as you explore with him his depths, you may find beauty and strength that neither you nor he dreamed could exist within him. And the moaning that we looked upon as a mere symptom of his misery may prove to be literally a breath of fresh air trying to make its way to the surface through all the misunderstandings of the years.

Persons who have become weary of the things that have kept their spontaneity in check and forced them to become dull and bored with life are often the ones you will meet in your study asking for help. The effort to change the habits of years may be too much for them, and they may realize that they cannot do it alone. It's then that they will seek out some minister they know, or whom a friend knows, or whom

41

they happen to pick out of the yellow pages of the phone book. If you, the chosen one, remember to look beneath the surface, you may find the real person who exists beneath all the subterfuges he feels it necessary to show as a front. Search for that "more than meets the eye" which is a part of every-one.

How are you to search?

For one thing, keep still and let the counselee do the talk-ing. Russell Dicks used to tell his classes, "Do no harm. That is the principle used by medical doctors. They believe that if you do not actually kill the patient Mother Nature will have a chance to cure him." So follow this cardinal rule in counsel-ing: "Do no harm."

Always remember that stream of fresh air from the inner-most caverns of the personality trying to make its way to the surface. You are not alone in the work you do. God has added his resources to the tools available to the minister; but for everyone who does counseling, the greatest ally of all is the counselee himself. He has a drive toward health that is always trying to make itself felt. In the depths of his personality, this drive is always trying to get a word through to you as you try to help him. The real person beneath the heaps of faulty, destructive experiences of his past life is still there as God made him, to be uncovered and restored to vitality by the skill of a loving counselor. If you cannot do that, at least do no harm. Leave the door open for someone else to try. If you slam the door in his face, he may go away disgusted not just with you, but with all counseling and all religion as well. That is why it is so important to make a minimum of mis-takes in dealing with the delicate material of which the human spirit is made.

What are the ways in which you could do harm and slam the door in the counselee's face?

One is by failing to recognize an opportunity when one

presents itself. A young minister at a youth camp came to me with this story:

"I am glad to be taking your course on counseling, for just before I came up here a woman in my church called me and demanded that I come out to her house immediately. She said she was desperate. I was desperate too, since I was an hour late for camp already, but she was so insistent that I went. I walked into the house telling her to make it brief, as I was in a tearing hurry. The story she told me was a wild one. She said her husband, who is a member of my board and whom I know pretty well, was running around with other women and that she had reached the point where she was going to commit either suicide or homicide or both. I told her to cut out the nonsense. Told her I knew her husband to be a fine man and that I was sure he was doing nothing of the kind. As for her talk of suicide and murder, I told her I thought that was just an attention-getting device. I told her to quit thinking about such things and I'd see her in church. Then I hurried off up here, but since I have been taking your course, I've been thinking to myself, you know—I bet that was a counseling situation."

Do not laugh too hard at the poor benighted counselor. Though his case is extreme, there are many who fail to recognize the seriousness of their counselee's needs.

At one hospital where I was chaplain, I visited Stella, who was the victim of not one but two ministers' failure to understand what she was trying to tell them. In her childhood Stella had found her father hanging from a rafter in the barn. He had committed suicide early that morning, but no one found him until Stella had walked in during her play. She had grown up with many conflicts in her attitudes toward men. Much against her mother's wishes, she had married a Catholic. Some years later a sister had come to live with her and had brought her little Scottie. Stella's husband, who did not like dogs, had never been fond of the

43

sister. One morning after a family row, her husband had gone out and kicked the sister's dog. In a fury of furies the sister had gone out to the garage and hanged herself. She, too, had been found by Stella who walked unsuspectingly into the garage later in the day. Apparently she held up under the experience fairly well. But suddenly the guilt of having married a Catholic began to plague her. She believed her husband had caused her sister's suicide, but she could not be angry because of her need to cling to her husband. So she appeared without warning at the church where she was active.

To the startled minister, she said, "I want to become a Catholic."

The minister was busy with the details of a Saturday afternoon, and he didn't like Catholics anyway. He flew into a fit of temper and said, "If that is the way you feel, do it. Don't tell me about it. However, we don't want any Catholic converts teaching our children, and since you are a teacher in the Sunday school I will ask you to turn in your material and I'll get a substitute for you tomorrow."

Crushed by this rejection, she went down to the Catholic priest where she got what seemed to her a very different reception.

"Fine," said the priest. "I am starting a new class of instruction on Monday morning, and you may get in right at the beginning."

Her husband was thrilled. Many years later, when I met her as a patient at the State Hospital, she remembered that day when she had decided to become a Catholic as the turning point of her life. As a matter of fact, both minister and priest did exactly the same thing to poor Stella. Both took what she said at face value and neither took the time or the interest in her as an individual to invite her to sit down for a moment and to ask her, "Now tell me, Stella, *why* do you want to become a Catholic?"

A second way to slam the door in a person's face is to give him advice. The dictionary definition of counseling includes the giving of advice, but I am inclined to agree with the old adage: "Advice can always be had for nothing, and it is usually worth it."

When we give advice to another, we do not get what we want or think we are getting. The person either takes our advice or he doesn't, with the result that he either blames us with a sour result or he feels no elation over a good result. The real goal of counseling is to help the person learn to make his own decisions and stand by the results of his own actions, neither alibiing nor shrugging off the responsibility.

"But," you protest, "won't they make mistakes?"

Of course they will make mistakes! Didn't your child fall down a few times when you were teaching him to walk? Didn't he gulp a few mouthfuls of water when you were teaching him to swim? Did you then carry him everywhere for the rest of his life? Did you refuse to let him go near the water ever after? It takes real self-control to let a counselee make mistakes. Often he will do the very opposite of what we think best, and many times the results will be tragic for him, but a wise counselor, like a wise parent, stands ready to help him pick up the pieces and start all over again. He does not save him from the results of his wrong choice. Faith is one of the most important tools in the counseling kit; faith in oneself, in one's counselee, in one's method of counseling, and faith in the God who made both counselor and counselee. Many persons experience real anxiety and confusion when you refuse to give the advice they expect and demand. The breaking-in period is a difficult one for both, but the rewards are great when the counselee finally learns the joy of free choice.

A third method of slamming the door in your counselee's face is, strangely enough, premature reassurance. Too many counselors do the most harm at this very point. Reassurance is a good thing. But when a person is suffering there is nothing that can do him as much good as allowing him to express his unhappiness to the full. He needs, more than anything else, to be heard out. To stand by sympathetically while one expresses his misery, and just *be there* without interrupting the flow of pain or anger, is the real secret and art of personal counseling. Only yesterday at a funeral, I heard a wise old family doctor say to a relative who was concerned that a mother would "make herself sick" because she was "crying too much" over the loss of her only son, "Let her alone. There's no tranquilizer that can do for her what she's doing right now for herself."

A fourth method of slamming the door in the face of the counselee is to make some expression of shock or disgust, or even enjoyment. There was a young girl student in training once who used to listen with obvious relish to the confessions of her patients, and if they told her a particularly racy bit of their past, she would breath rapturously, *"No kidding."*

To join in the recriminations of the counselee, to flare up with anger, or to weep bitter tears yourself will not help, neither will a self-righteous horror at the things the counselees say or the way they say them. The language of those who suffer may not be allowed on television, but it must be allowed in your office if you are to assure the person that you can like him even when he does not like himself. Your need to take a stand is one of the occupational hazards of the minister who also does counseling. Not only ministers, but doctors also find it hard to take when the patient expresses himself in crude or profane language. I remember an interview Lucy Fine, a little woman doctor in a state hospital, once had with a patient.

"I think I'll throw this damn coffee right in your face," said the patient.

"If you do, you'll get shock treatment," said Dr. Fine.

She thus effectively slammed the door in the patient's face.

Usually any outburst on the part of the counselor reflects his own emotional problems rather than those of the patient. The counselee then becomes frightened or angry and withdraws. Never forget that there is more here than meets the eye, and hear your counselee out even if your own feelings do get a bit out of hand. Act out an indifference you do not feel, and hear him out rather than speak and frighten him away. Remember that your counselee is suffering beyond your power to comprehend, and suppress the tendency to moralize, which is after all just another way of slamming the door in his face.

The best of us have blind spots exactly where our own problems and those of our counselees meet. So keep a sharp eye on your own reactions at all times. If you find yourself becoming emotional over your counselee's problems, let it be a flashing yellow light in your brain—there may be danger ahead for both of you. If you are inclined to weep over the problems of another or get excessively angry over something he says or does or reports said or done, watch it! Tell yourself, "In this area I too must have problems."

You do not need to present the picture of an unfeeling robot; you only need to be sympathetic and understanding without becoming involved in the problems of your counselee or entangled in his emotional storms.

Sometimes you may be tempted to "help" by telling him how you helped another man with the same difficulty, or how you solved exactly the same thing in your own life. Your counselee believes, and may even tell you, that no one has ever suffered as he is suffering now, and that no problem is similar to his. When you start slamming the door in this way you will see a look of boredom cross his face, and he will soon find an excuse to leave.

One of the most understandable ways in which a minister is tempted to slam the door is by becoming impatient. If someone is late or fails to show up at all, or if he arrives but sits in sullen or frightened silence for the entire forty-five minutes, you can certainly be forgiven a furtive glance at the numerous tasks waiting to be tackled. You may even get a little resentful. The multiplicity of your duties staggers you, and here sits this man gabbing about some triviality, or just sitting there silent.

I once had a student who told me, "When someone comes to me for counseling and then refuses to talk, I simply tell him that though he can afford to waste his time, I cannot afford to waste mine. I then turn to the telephone or the dictating machine and proceed to get my church work done."

He had no intention of hurting his counselee, for I knew him to be a very kind man. It simply had not occurred to him that the confessions of troubled people do not come easy, that they are quite painful, and that one must feel extremely welcome in the minister's office before he will bare his soul to view and perhaps to criticism. There is usually a large proportion of guilt feeling in the reasons that brought him to you in the first place—he expects to be condemned, so he remains silent trying to work up the courage to speak of these things that cause him to feel so guilty. To be condemned for that very silence is to be condemned before one has even begun! If your counselee expects you to condemn him and you do so, you have confirmed his worst fears about himself.

Even when your counselee demands that you condemn him, as some will by telling you the worst thing they can think of to tell you about themselves, your cue is to withhold judgment until you discover what it is that he is really saying to you. It may be something quite different from the "confession" with which he began. A depressed woman, for example, may confess to having kissed the milkman twenty years ago. She may or may not have kissed the milkman, but the chances are that the event has no bearing on her mood of depression at the present time. It is only a test of your tolerance. Be patient. Do not condemn. And you will be rewarded. She is merely making an effort to communicate. She is not stubbornly withholding information. It behooves us to remember that what the counselee states as truth, he believes to *be* truth. If it were not so, our task would be a great deal simpler. An attitude of complete acceptance and understanding which is more than just sympathy is the deepest need of the counselee. If he finds that he can be accepted with all his unacceptable thoughts and feelings, perhaps he can begin to accept himself. Only as he is able to believe that his counselor accepts him and, through the confidence the counselor inspires in him, to begin to accept himself a little, will he be able to believe in the acceptance and forgiveness of God.

Thus, in a certain sense, like the old-time witch doctor, we are taking the place of God when we attempt to counsel another. Our attitude toward the person represents to him the attitude that God would take if he were in the office. If our attitude is condemnatory and short-sighted, if we jump to conclusions and give hasty advice, the counselee will go away disgusted, not just with us, but with God too, and even more, with himself. If we can be tolerant, accepting of the person's feelings, he may learn that however wicked his past, there is a God who understands, loves, forgives, and reconstructs. But it is necessary that one have a human hand to guide, before one can reach this deeper atonement. Such a hand is provided by the counselor who looks ever for that "more than meets the eye," which awaits discovery in the deeper caverns of the human spirit.

Be patient. Keep silent. Listen.

For what? The person himself does not know, yet he is the only one who does know. How can you know?

There is more.

49

How much more? What?

The realization that he needs help comes only from the symptoms of his real trouble.

How can you handle it all?

Will you help these people? Or will you hurt them more than you will help them?

Do not fear your ineffectiveness. If you are genuinely interested in another person, he will know it. There is a certain feeling tone, which some call nonverbal communication and others call intuition or telepathy and still others call instinct—it is that awareness which makes a child or an animal know whether he is in the presence of a friend or an enemy. The feeling tone and the counselee's great need will keep him coming back for what you have that makes him feel better. If you keep quiet, he will work out his own problems in spite of your errors.

"But," you say, "that is just it. How can I know whether I am keeping quiet at the right times?"

In the following chapters, I will outline briefly the development of the child and his emotional life and explain how the events of childhood affect later feelings and actions. There may be times when you think I am describing you instead of your counselee. As a matter of fact, I *am* describing every human being in the world. The strange elements that go into the making of an individual may be rejected, but they can never be forgotten. If you become angry or shocked at certain statements in the following pages, there's that flashing yellow light again. It is just at those points that you yourself may have strong feelings relating to forgotten events in your own life.

Counseling is a thrilling experience for those who give as well as those who get it. Your fears of failure merely serve to make you cautious. If you have a bit of hesitance, remember that your counselee will help you to help him. In the end, you will find that nothing is hidden by his fears and anxieties that shall not be revealed in the sacred temple of the confessional, and that every new revelation of the unknown caverns of his soul will bring relief to his troubled spirit, and joy and inspiration to your own.

3

It Doth Not Yet Appear What We Shall Be

"Mother, someone was here yesterday—all day. She looked exactly like you but she wasn't you."

"Who was she, Janey dear?"

"I don't know her—she yelled at me, and when I yelled back at her she hit me. Stay with me today, Mother, I don't want *her* to come back." Trusting blue eyes looked up into startled blue eyes.

Across town brown eyes stared up into blazing brown ones.

"There was a girl once. She used to live with us. She was so nice. Her name was Maxine."

Maxine turned away.

"Can I be that bad?" she asked herself.

The next day in my office she wept as she told me, "Doris stamped her foot at me and screamed, 'You're a witch! I hate you!' and I spanked her! I know I just confirmed it. Now *I* think I'm a witch too. *Why? Why?*"

"You mean why does Doris think you are a witch or why *are* you one?"

The comment said with a smile deliberately begs the question "Why do I do it?" in order to give Maxine time to luxuriate in her moment of self-condemnation. She may be experiencing some legitimate guilt over her treatment of Doris and need to suffer a little; at the same time I am reassuring her by my teasing attitude and my smile that I do not consider the whole thing the major tragedy she does.

But the question comes to my own mind, "Why a witch?" Why does Doris call her mother one? Why does Maxine agree with her? Was the "stranger" in Janey's house a witch too?

In the first chapter we learned that the history of witches is a long one. Now we come to look at the witch in the nursery. The universal appeal of such stories as Snow White in which we find a dear dead mother and a jealous stepmother; or Cinderella with the wicked stepmother and the fairy godmother; or even Red Riding Hood in which the dear old grandmother turns out at last to be a wolf, indicates that all of us have been confused at times by the changing moods of our parents. To bring reason into the confusion the child simply makes two people out of one: if mother is in the mood for loving and giving she is the fairy godmother, if she is in a rejecting, withholding, and cross mood she is the wicked witch. When the mother takes care of the child's needs and satisfies his demands she is the good mother, but when she refuses his demands and takes her time about feeding the child she is the wicked witch.

Time passes, and the child forgets he ever thought of his mother as two people. Which one is the "forgotten" mother depends on the prevailing mood of the real mother. If she is predominantly loving and giving, the fantasy of the witch gradually fades from the child's mind; but if she is pre-dominantly rejecting and hateful, the image of the good mother fades away. But the idea of making two people for opposing moods does not entirely fade away. Rather than try to cope with the opposite feelings of love and hate toward the same person, we enter into a folk fantasy of two mothers, two fathers, even two children ("That's not mother's good little girl").

The most important year of anyone's life is the year in which he is born. During that year his body takes shape and is formed in the direction of his life, as does his person-ality. In order to build a strong body, he must eat well. Since eating is the most important thing he does during his first twelve months, the emotions and feelings that surround the eating process follow him through life. Certainly the in-stinct of self-preservation is worth a great deal to the race as well as to the individual. Essential to remaining alive is the business of eating. During his first few months the baby wakes and eats and sleeps only to wake and eat.

Along with his eating, other things are taking place even though the infant is at best only dimly aware of them. His sense of smell develops. The odors of his mother come to him quite vividly. The personality of his mother is conveyed to him in innumerable small ways—the way she holds him, for example. If her touch is warm, loving, and accepting it gives him a feeling that all is well; if, on the other hand, she holds him in a tense and anxious fashion he reacts in a tense and nervous way. He is not aware that he is smelling, hear-ing, eating, and intuiting his mother all at the same time. He just considers it all a part of the act of eating.

He believes that he is eating up his mother even though he is actually becoming aware of her through all his five senses and through another more subtle medium of aware-ness which gives him the aforementioned sense of warmth and well-being or tense anxiety. All of the feeling tone that represents his mother to him gives him the false impression that she herself has entered into him by way of his mouth. He cannot be expected to understand that all the things that are his mother are being taken in through his five senses plus a certain intuition that tells him his mother either loves or doesn't love him. He only knows that when he eats, his mother is present. After he has eaten, his mother goes away and his stomach feels full. In the strange unreasoning perception that is infantile thinking, the child believes that his mother is inside his stomach.

The fantasy of the two mothers is only one of the strange fantasies of childhood. When one is too little to talk and ask questions, but not too young to think and imagine, he tends to make up answers to his own questions. So when later he ejects this mass of food from his little stomach and feels hungry, and when he cries or calls his mother and she returns, he believes that he has eaten her and passed her in the form of feces and that here she is revived again!

And now you are wondering, "How can anyone think anything so foolish. It is incredible!" We may say so, but is it any more incredible than the adult fantasy that the child is so "innocent" he does not know anything about the "facts of life"? He who from the beginning has been interested in just one thing, the body and its functions! Just as the primary colors are red, blue, and yellow, and all others are shades and mixtures of these three, so a child's interests are love, hate, and the bodily functions not only of himself but also of those closest to him—mother, father, brother, sister; and all else in life for as far as it goes on is merely a variation on these themes.

Knowing this, it is easier to understand Joe who sits miserably in a chair in the church office staring at you. "I have been reading some in the Einstein theory of relativity," he begins, "and I am afraid it is beginning to interfere with my faith in God and the eternal verities. I had a simple faith

55

in the doctrine my mother taught me, and I cannot reconcile it with this bit about relativity."

How tempting it is to launch into a discussion of the theory of relativity! How great it would be to show the extent of your own erudition on the subject! But hold everything. Remember that this man has retained his primary interest in love, hate, and the bodily functions, and try this:

"Your mother taught you what you believe about your faith?" Now you are steering him in the direction that will lead to his real problem. It becomes second nature to pick out of a conversation the mention of relatives, loved ones, and feelings. All we have to do is lift out an elemental subject, and we get a response like I did from this man Joe:

"She sure did, and now she wants to marry a Jewish rabbi and join the synagogue. I've been so upset I've had diarrhea for three days, and this morning I threw up my breakfast."

You see, it wasn't relativity. Joe did not appear to be primarily interested in the bodily functions and sensations of eating and eliminating, nor in the loves and hates of the members of his immediate family, but he was; and until you learn to look for these from the very first moment your visitor enters your office you have not learned the rudiments of counseling.

"The child is father to the man," said Wordsworth, and it would be good for us to remember as we begin our study of counseling that every man is fathered by a child, that every individual who comes to the minister's office was born an infant.

The more we understand of the growth and development of children and how people express what they are in every tiny act they perform, the more we are intrigued by the intuitive wisdom of the great writers of all the ages. For the child is indeed father to the man in many ways in which our English professors never told us.

Humperdinck's opera *Hansel and Gretel* is performed every

Christmas, and it never seems to lose its charm. It is based on a folktale that is frankly concerned with eating up, killing, and reviving one's relatives. Children talk quite freely about killing and eating various members of their families or their little friends. Of course, they later revive these victims of their cannibalism. They do not understand until much later in life the real meaning of death. In the story of Hansel and Gretel there are two mothers, the good mother of the home and the bad mother of the forest. It is the real mother who temporarily rejects the children, but they cannot believe that their "good" mother would do such a thing so they run away and spend the night in the lonely forest getting what comfort they can from each other's presence. (What a familiar little domestic scene this is! It happens somewhere in your congregation every night. Mother becomes tired and angry and rejects the kids. Even the bedroom seems like a lonely forest when mother's love is absent, but the little ones derive what comfort they can from each other.)

Next morning mamma is worse than ever. She's a real bearcat today. She's so bad that she bakes little boys and girls and eats them with the gingerbread. She locks up protector brother and ties him with a string (apron string?), but sister lets him out. Suddenly they learn that in numbers there is strength. They rescue the other children, and together they shove the witch into her own oven; the gingerbread children come back to life. Into the forest clearing come the revived good mother and father, and all the children dance around them as the curtain falls.

When an adult comes seeking help, he is not thinking of such things. Long ago he must have realized that his mother was one person and not two. Yes, he must have, but did he? Listen to him:

"My mother would never marry a rabbi! *Never!* There's something wrong with her. The Bible talks about demon-possession. Do you think it is possible that my mother could be possessed of the devil and that he is telling her to marry this man? My father was a *good* man—and he was a *Christian*. How can she do it to his memory? It would break his heart!"

"You mean it's breaking *your* heart?" Ask it gently—this man is hurting.

"Yes, I mean it's breaking my heart! [shouting.] I thought I meant something to her. I gave up everything for her. After Daddy died I quit school and got a job. I even gave up my own chances for marriage. *I* was in love once."

He breaks down and weeps at the thought of how unimportant he is at last to her.

Fantastic as it seems, you must remember that this man who came to you with Einstein's theory and is now raving about the marriage plans of his mother is beset by the same unreasoning fears, bewildered by the same unexplained misunderstandings, shuddering at the same primitive terrors, and tortured by the same loneliness as the unloved child. Many years ago his reason grew up. He would be the first to agree that he does not think of the childhood dreams he had when his father died, though later he may remember some of them as vividly as if it were only yesterday, but he is talking now about his mother, who seems to be a stranger to him, and of his alimentary canal and of his shattered self-love. Thus the fantastic savage world of the infant becomes covered and hidden from view by the subterfuges and oblique confessions of the adult. It is a wise counselor who can uncover the real meaning beneath the veneer of culture.

"I feel like going out and getting roaring drunk," your counselee is saying, and you know what he means.

This man has never lost the feeling that his oral needs are all-important. You remember others like him. When the boss bawls him out or his wife is cold and unfriendly, he seeks out the first handy bottle and thrusts it into his mouth. He feels he is too grown-up to get a milk bottle, so he makes it a liquor bottle. If he is obese he casts discretion to the winds and goes after another chicken leg. Either way he is punishing himself and gratifying (or over-gratifying) his oral needs at the same time. Whether he goes for the liquor bottle or the milk bottle your counselee is attempting to satisfy a deep and abiding hunger for love—a hunger that cannot be satisfied by eating and drinking. He will tell you eventually that this is not the first time he has been hurt by his mother, that he believes his father was hurt by her more than once. He may go on to say that he never felt really welcome in his own home, to explain that all his "sacrifices" for his mother were done grudgingly and with resentment. At last he may say:

"I'm really glad to get rid of the old girl, but it grinds me to see her take all that money we have saved together, and I think the man is really only interested in her money— *our money.*"

Now he is getting honest with himself, and soon he will accept the marriage and his new freedom with gladness. But don't think he's safe home. He may then have a reaction of guilt for all the mean things he has said and need your support even more as he finishes belatedly cutting the cord.

These things, you notice, I say he *may* tell you. He may not. Certainly not if you do not know what to watch for and stop on the first level with a discussion of relativity.

Now, having insisted you look beyond what *seems* to be troubling the counselee into the things that are possible, I must go back a little and say "it ain't necessarily so." Walking down a city street, you see three balls hanging out over a storefront, but this does not inevitably mean you are approaching a pawn shop. You could find as you get nearer that it is abandoned, burned out, or the guy just likes three balls hanging out over the door. But the chances are quite good that your first guess is correct. It is good to be always thinking of what the counselee may tell you next, but do not become addicted to your own predictions. That is exactly when he will surprise you. Your visitor may be motivated by many other unconscious fantasies about which you will want to learn more.

Each fantasy is developed in connection with a bodily function—the fantasy of the two mothers comes during the time when the most important bodily function is eating. Some people even believe that the idea of two mothers developed from the physical fact that mother has two breasts, or "feeding stations" as some children love to call them. Along with eating goes defecating, and with defecating goes killing and reviving. At each level of the child's development come new problems to be solved, new ideas, new needs. Not all our needs are met by even the best of parents, and so we have frustrations and angers developing along the way.

In the Muir Woods is a cross section of a giant redwood tree with tabs on its rings to indicate its age. One such tab marks the Battle of Hastings, 1066; another, the birth of Jesus; still another, the building of Solomon's Temple. Not only can we trace the history of the world by the rings, but also the history of the individual tree—dry years leave thin rings; years with heavy rains leave fat rings. Like the rings of a tree are the years of our lives.

Whether pleasant or unpleasant in their effects, all the stages of childhood leave an indelible impression never to be forgotten. A person does not remember with the detailed imagery of an adult mind the things that happened to him in the first days and weeks of his life. The world of the child is remembered by his feelings. Early emotions are expressed later as attitudes, and reactions to events. Since we remember not so much with our reason as with our feeling, we respond to people and events, to circumstances, sights and sounds, even to smells, as if we were still children. The redwood tree, through its rings, showed the scars of its history. With us humans, too, the final result is implicit in the beginning.

Some adults seem to think of a baby as more animal than man, but an infant is not an animal—he is a small human being. He shows his humanity in many ways. Any parent can tell you that a child is quite an individual, even at birth.

First of all our infant is a little bundle of "*I want.*" All he knows is bound up in his own needs, mostly the needs of his alimentary canal. He knows when he is hungry, he knows when he wants to urinate or defecate, he knows when he is cold (he is seldom hot). These very personal wants comprise his complete and total interest.

The counselee is first of all interested in his Personal comfort. If he is uncomfortable physically, he will be less able to talk freely. We get him a comfortable lounge chair; give him a hassock to prop his feet on; put a box of Kleenex at his elbow, and be sure the bathroom is handy, the light not glaring in his eyes, and no undue noises distracting his attention. With all the minutiae that sometimes seem unnecessary to you as a new counselor, you provide this now-grown baby with the security that he learned to appreciate in the first days of his life. He may be extremely uncomfortable emotionally, but if he is comfortable physically, he will be better able to keep his mind on the problem that brought him to you in the first place.

During the first weeks and months of life the child wants, and usually gets, food. His mother is his constant servant. How can she know when he is hungry? Or wet? Or sleepy? Yet she is always there meeting his needs, so there arises another fantasy—he is an omnipotent king. Remember Narcissus of Greek mythology, who saw his own image reflected in a pool and became so enamored of himself that he fell in the water and drowned? Such self-love is called original sin by some Christians. I do not like the term original sin because it carries a stigma of evil, and to love oneself is not evil, though to love oneself to excess is disastrous to all other human relationships. Some self-love is necessary to life. The person who does not love himself at all finds a way to commit suicide. How can we love our neighbor as ourselves if we do not love ourselves? All of life is predicated on the principle that what we do brings us happiness and comfort. Good things come our way, and we immediately devise ways of making these good things more numerous and the times when they come more frequent. Life can go on only insofar as one derives some measure of peace and comfort from it. There are many variations on the theme, and we must learn to recognize them all.

I remember Eileen, the first baby to be born into the family for fourteen years. It was Christmastime, and everyone was standing about the piano singing carols while Grandma accompanied. Eileen was brought downstairs, and immediately she burst into violent screaming.

"What's the matter with the baby?"

"Well, you gotta admit we're pretty bad."

"We're no opera singers, but is she a critic?"

"Maybe Eileen will grow up to be one."

Grandma interprets: "No, I've got it. This is the first time in her little life she has ever come downstairs without making a grand entry. She's not a critic, she's a prima donna. Every prima donna hates the chorus. It's our fault. We always stop everything and make over her; she thinks it's her right. For once we are more interested in one another and our singing than we are in her, and her feelings are hurt."

"This will be only the first of a series of jolts—wait till she goes to school."

"Or until she has a little brother."

"Now *just a minute!*" (From Eileen's forty-two-year-old mother.)

In all of us, if we are normal, the feeling of omnipotence is shaken by the time we are one year of age or shortly thereafter.

In one sense of the word, the term normal might be used

synonymously with timely. It is natural and right and appropriate for an infant to be self-centered; it is harmful to himself and others for a man of fifty to be self-centered. It is normal enough for a baby to prefer most of his nourishment in liquid form; it is tragic for a man of forty-five to do so!

One of the ways in which the change from omnipotence to realism takes place is through the development of teeth. I remember a friend of mine who said she was lying half asleep and the baby was nursing when suddenly he bit her, and she slapped him. He screamed out in fear and pain, waking his mother who then felt extremely guilty. Thus the child begins to realize that, in this world of his, other people have feelings and that he has weapons to arouse those feelings. He learns that the weapons in his mouth can be quite painful to his mother, and he both fears and enjoys his budding sadism. But because he feels at times that he would like to bite and eat up the breast of the mother, he also fears that *it* would like to bite and eat *him* up!

One of the greatest misconceptions of all adult life is the belief that other people feel toward us just exactly as we feel toward them. No greater falsehood could ever be imagined. Each person feels and thinks for himself, each in his own way, each in a different way; and no one person echoes the feelings of another exactly. You will meet this attitude often in counseling. Never assume that you know what your patron feels or thinks—ask him.

"How does that make you feel? What are you thinking?"

And if he says, "You know what I mean?" never carelessly say "Yes"; instead be honest.

"No, what do you mean?"

His answer may surprise you. This mechanism of projection follows us through life, beginning when the infant is so small that there is no possibility of reasoning with him. Yet the mechanism has its value too. Else how would one ever be able to put himself in another's place? The counselee who thinks all people hate him and the counselor who sympathizes and understands both use the mechanism of projection—one in a sick way, the other in a healing way.

"My mother isn't happy; I know she isn't." (Your relativity friend is back.) "Last night I had dinner with them—and Mother took pains to hold that old man's hand and kiss the top of his bald head. She has never been demonstrative—I know she's trying to convince herself."

"You mean you miss her?"

"Of course, I miss her! Why are you always telling me something I know already?"

Inwardly you sigh. You thought you had him all settled. He was enjoying his newfound freedom, he had been dating, and yet here he is projecting again.

Once in awhile you get a visit from a person who needs only one problem cleared up, but only once in awhile. Most of the time they keep coming back. That one person can be helped by a few interviews does not mean that most can. Let me emphasize over and over that you must not expect quick results nor feel your job is done if one problem is resolved.

"I think with my help the patient has gotten worse," a student said to me once. It may seem that way at times. But if we are patient and don't slam the door . . .

Remember we talked earlier about slamming the door in your counselee's face? A way not to slam the door is to understand all the things that may have affected the life of the individual and all the possible "hang-ups" he could have, and wait. If you have helped him once, and if he does not feel at peace with himself, he will come back for more.

Love and acceptance will melt away the fear, the hate, the antisocial behavior as nothing else can, but it takes time. It usually takes a long, long time. Many ministers and other professionals get discouraged with the time it takes and give up the attempt or try to short-cut the procedure. But think of the time it takes to rear a child. Consider that he has learned how to relate to people "all wrong," and remember something you have learned to do wrong. Take golf or bowling, for example, and try to recall how long it takes to eliminate a slice or a left hook, once acquired, and you can imagine how long it will take to remold this personality warped from birth by ignorant, neurotic, or even actively hostile parents. Yes, love can cure all things, but not in a day.

Joe is a strong man, but he weeps as he talks about a beating he had taken as a child.

"How can they beat a little child? Can I be crying for myself? It was so long ago. But this is true of other children too. These stupid parents are so angry, and all their lives they have been waiting to unload this huge burden of hatred on their helpless child—all that anger and frustration. And that's because their parents unloaded *their* anger on them, and theirs on them. Will it ever end?"

"Yes, it began to end a bit ago when you came to me." This is no time to let him luxuriate in his misery. Joe is suffering now to the extent that he needs some comfort and encouragement.

A little later he says: "I think I have never understood the passages relating to 'the sins of the fathers' before. Somehow I feel better about God now. I feel less puzzled, more secure. God isn't just a harsh old judge who won't forgive for generations on end because he's vindictive. The scriptures are just telling it like it is."

Many scriptures gain fresh meaning to your counselees as they talk over their lives with you. Joe began to see that we are born in one time and place, to one set of parents. We are one race and color at birth which nothing can change, and we are one sex which no one has yet successfully changed. We are of a nationality, a social stratum, an economic level— all not of our doing. The color of our eyes and hair, the strength and endurance of our bodies are inherited, but much of our attitude toward life which seems to be inborn is learned from the place and time in which we were born, from our circumstances and the folk culture of the family into which we were born. It was this that made him understand one of the apparently cruel scriptures:

> It is the Eternal, the Eternal, a God pitiful and kind, slow to be angry, rich in love and loyalty, proving kind to thousands, forgiving iniquity and transgression and sin, but one who will never acquit the guilty, one who avenges the sins of fathers on their children and their children's children, down to the third and the fourth generation.
>
> (Exod. 34:6-7 Moffatt.)

As are so many scriptures, this is realistic rather than cruel. Regardless of how little we like it there are many people who are doomed to failure or to poverty or to misery because that is all they have ever known. Their parents have taught them how to fail, to be on welfare, to be poor or miserable, and they need you and me to help them learn a new way of life.

One of my best friends is a minister in a large city church. He tells of his boyhood in St. Louis: "My brother and I were just nuts about baseball. We tried to get our schoolwork done every day in time to listen to the game on the radio, and nothing could get us away from it once the game had started. Yet it never occurred to us that we could take our fifty cents and go out to the ball park and *watch* the Cards play! We were raised to think of ourselves as just little people and as poor but honest people, and such luxuries as actually watching a ball game were for the rich and powerful, not for people like us!"

This is the opposite of that narcissicism we talked about earlier. There are those who take pride in their dejected state. One man in ten may overcome such a handicap as did my friend, but many are visited by the sins of their fathers in such a way that they pass it on to the third and fourth generation. In our next chapter we shall see how "the sins of the fathers" produce many of the wars, campus riots, church splits, and divorces that plague the time in which we live.

4
Cain Slew His Brother

Down the ages rings the mighty voice of God: "Where is thy brother?"

And the defiant sneer of Cain echoes its eternal answer: "Am I my brother's keeper?"

To say, "Yes, you are your brother's keeper," is too simple. The feelings of Cain represent a universal experience. If you can't believe it, listen. Listen to your children and your neighbor's children, and listen to your own heart also, and you will have proof enough that brotherly hatred dwells in the unknown depths of everyone. Much as you might *want* to be your brother's keeper, your dislike of him keeps getting in the way.

"Ah, my Carmen," wails Don José as he bends over the

body of the love he has just killed, and the whole world weeps with him.

Delilah destroys the strength of Samson.

Jael drives a spike through the head of Sisera.

Esther trembles with fear as she asks a favor of Ahasuerus, even though she knows she is his favorite wife. The universal appeal of such stories brings into sharp focus the dichotomy of the human heart that causes us to feel both love and hate for one person, often at the same time.

Frustration develops in a world where there never is enough love to go around. Frustration combined with natural aggressiveness produces hostility. Even so, all that we look upon as success requires the application of well-placed aggression. Without it no cities would be built, no elections won, no treaties written, no music composed. Without aggression we would never get out of bed in the morning! Even at play a certain amount of aggression is necessary to success. But if every effort at expressing aggressive feelings is struck down in childhood, then we begin to look on all aggressive acts as "bad." The sad result may be total inertia or the most common form of perverted aggressiveness in which the person puts forth great effort to be "nice" for as long as he can stand himself in the role and then explodes into violence, followed by guilt. How many families do you know in which this pattern is repeated? They are polite to one another for a few days or weeks, then they have a fine big family fight. Everybody cries, they make up, and then they start all over again. How like our society this is, how like our churches!

In the family of nations also we proclaim our love for peace and give to the underprivileged peoples of the world as long as we can bear it—then we blow each other up (literally), repent, form another world organization for peace, and start over. The need to express one's pent-up hostilities takes many forms. One of the hindrances to success in life is the need constantly to deny our own aggression.

69

We preach peace and make war. We cut our neighbor's throat in a business deal and talk about our business ethics. We knee our opponent in a ball game and brag of sportsmanship.

Where does it all start? In the cradle. And right there in the cradle is where it can be stopped.

My friend Norma, mother of five, expressed it beautifully in her Christmas note:

"After pounding many pillows substituting for Margie (the baby), shocking older friends with words of dislike about her, Heidi said several months ago, 'I'm really glad we've got her after all. She's fun!'

"They play for hours without quarreling. She helps dress Margie, 'baby-sits' in the car with her. Young parents tell us how free from jealousy their next-eldest children are when cherubs arrive. Maybe most parents *need* five before being willing to admit the green-eyed monster cleaves even to *their* children!" She goes on to describe her own: "Dealing realistically with it, for us, means allowing the elder child to express resentment verbally, without fear of censorship, and by substitution of a poundable object for the unpoundable baby. The eldest, when restrained from too much teasing of his younger sisters, sighed, 'Wish I was an only child,' but next week exclaimed, 'Oh, golly, why don't we have a baby this year!' He feels guilty because he resents them and perplexed because he enjoys them."

Thus does she express with rare insight the sibling feelings of us all. She is one in a million.

Put yourself in Heidi's place for a moment and take a look at this new baby from her point of view. Let us say that she has had the most admirable preparation for Margie's arrival. She has looked forward to having a new baby in the family with a great deal of expectation and pleasure. No matter how much she has looked forward to it, however, the fact remains that her mother, whose undivided attention she has had throughout her life, suddenly must devote the major portion of her activities to a squirming brat not half so intelligent or so interesting as herself.

Heidi has been expecting another child with whom to play—have not her parents been saying, "We are having another baby because we want Heidi to have someone smaller to share with"? But who can play with this? This intruder, this nuisance, this rival for the affection of her mother and father, this disturber of the peace, this night screamer, this bed-wetter, this *thing!* To love her! She does well not to murder her!

Sometimes she tries. Of course, in a few months her hopes of a playmate will be realized, but months are like years to a child. At present the baby who was to have been hers to play with is nothing but trouble, and Heidi reacts to this new frustration, as she has reacted to earlier frustrations, with anger. Heidi is a lucky little girl to have a mother as tolerant and understanding as Norma. The chances are good that she will learn to tolerate her own negative feelings without undue anxiety!

It is the unusual mother who can rescue the infant from the gouging fingers, the exploring hands, the murderous milk bottle wielded like a sledgehammer without becoming upset herself. Being rare and wise, Norma expects these evidences of real feeling on the part of the older children, accepts them, and protects the baby from them without at the same time making Heidi and the others feel that they have committed the unpardonable sin.

Average parents seem to find difficulty in accepting the hostilities of their offspring. It is the wise mother and the rare one who can say, as Norma does, "We never interfere until the blood flies." Let the children fight it out, and they will usually arrive at a more or less peaceful solution. Of course this is not possible when one of them is still in the cradle.

Nothing is more attractive to a child than a younger, smaller child. Heidi will soon learn to love the baby, but she does not love her by instinct. She does not always understand that the younger baby has feelings. She treats her as she would treat a puppy or a kitten—squeezing it, slamming it around, pinching it, exploring it to see if it will squeak and being delighted when it does, but having absolutely no conception of the real meaning of those frantic squeaks. So Norma protects each child from the other in these early months. Heidi she protects from the disaster of feeling left out, abandoned, misunderstood, unloved. Margie she protects from the sadistic impulses of Heidi and the others. She may not succeed one hundred percent, but she will have some charming experiences while she tries.

There is unfortunately a theory floating about that to express honest anger, indignation, or even aggression is "sinful" and "unchristian." Such is not the case if by Christian we mean behavior like that of Jesus. It is true that he said, "Love your enemies," and the love of one's enemies is still good—*and easy* if we understand the motivation back of their annoying behavior. But Jesus never balked at the expression of honest anger. He threw the money changers out of the temple. He called the scribes and Pharisees dirty names. When his own mother got officious, took advantage of her position as the mother of a great man, or tried to run his life, as mothers will, she got sat on—hard.

"Woman, what have I to do with thee?" he said when she told him what to do about the wine at the wedding in Cana. Like many a grown son after him he went ahead and did it, but first he let mama know how he felt about being told.

Even at the age of twelve he shows an adolescent independence: "Wist ye not that I must be about my Father's business?" he says to his father and mother.

In later years when he is a grown man (his father, by implication, long since dead), his mother and brothers decide he is offending too many people; he must be mad. They decide to "put him away," and they send for him. Can't you just see the imperious, well-meaning mother using the other siblings to back her up in getting her way with her recalcitrant son? But he never leaves his post at all. "Who is my mother?" he inquires. "Who are my brothers?" After a man is grown his true brethren are those who understand and appreciate him—not his blood kin, whom all too often he has outgrown. His tender solicitude for his mother as he hangs on the cross is not at variance with this attitude— one can love even more the mother from whom one has had the courage to declare his independence. A great Protestant leader once said, "There is a big difference between Jesus and a doormat." Yet all too often this side of the Master's personality is glossed over or ignored. To become an independent person in one's own right, a certain amount of aggression is essential. When aggression is constantly beaten down it becomes imbued with bitterness and smolders with an intensity all the greater because it hides behind a smiling face. Even the writer of Proverbs tells us, "He that hideth hatred with lying lips . . . is a fool." (Proverbs 10:18).

During the first two years, when a child's mind is not fully developed, he is expected to recapitulate the entire social development of the race. Savage that he is at heart, we expect him to learn to wear clothes, eat with awkward utensils, dodge cars, ride trikes, love God, respect elders, obey parents, love younger children, take turns, share, keep neat toilet habits. All this we take for granted. The astounding thing is that he attacks his tasks with cheerfulness and enthusiasm. That is, if he is given love and encouragement along the way. No wonder they call this time of life "The Terrible Twos"! The poor little thing has so much demanded of him that he is naturally frustrated and angry. Of course he says "no" to everything. He won't have to learn so many new things in the four years of college as he does during his first two years

73

of life. If his mother is wise, she does not demand too much of her little savage.

Observe the cat with her kittens. She comes into the nest and she sprawls out. The kittens crawl all over her, they paw her, they lick her, they drink her milk, they slap at her with their little claws, they play with one another. She shows not a shred of anxiety about them. She allows everything—anything goes except real physical danger to an individual kitten. That brings action. But no demands are made on these kittens. If they crawl into a dangerous place she retrieves them, but she does not expect of them wisdom beyond their little weeks; she does not slap their paws because they crawl out over the floor furnace! If a child is brought up by a mother who can be as relaxed as a cat, he is a pretty healthy baby!

In every group there is invariably a problem of readjustment when a new member arrives. It is as true in the home as it is in our family of nations.

Perhaps the emotion we fear most and understand least is anger. A good parent, usually the father, teaches the child early in life to express his aggression in such a way that he succeeds without being offensive. To be friendly with one's anger is to be mature. Dad recongizes that a certain amount of aggression is necessary to life, and he teaches the child to use this God-given quality.

The Macs were all in the backyard. and Richard was reporting a neighborhood squabble to Dad: "You know what? Masie hit Nan four times [Masie is the neighbor, Nan the sister], and when I hit Masie for hitting Nan, Masie cried and said *I* hit *her* four times." He squared off indignantly.

"I hope Nan didn't cry," said Dad, eyeing his daughter.

"She didn't. She hit Masie right back."

"Good girl!" said Dad approvingly.

Nan looked smug while Mother laughed contentedly from

the porch steps. "The fighting Macs, that's what he'd like to have us called," she said, smiling adoringly at Dad.

Thus encouraged, children learn to defend themselves without developing feelings of neurotic guilt.

Another member of the family explained it in a conversation with a small friend.

"I hate Mother!" said Joe.

"Oh, Joe, you don't *hate* your *mother!*" said his playmate in an awed tone.

"Yeah, I do too," said Joe casually. "I asked her to drive me to town, and she said she didn't have time. When she won't do what I want her to, I hate her."

It was as simple as that. And that is what hostility is on its most primary level—hostility means no more than that—when someone will not do what we want him to we hate him. When he does what we like, we love him. On the really primitive level of childhood this is the whole story of love and hate in a nutshell.

Love and hate are not opposites. They live and grow side by side. It is not accurate to say that one loves or one hates any given individual. We can only say that we have strong feelings about that individual. Hate and love go together. Like the two sides of a coin, they are inseparable.

Marty was a patient assigned to me in my first quarter of training. She had once been a beautiful woman, and still she dressed tastefully if a bit flamboyantly. Today her red hair was piled up high. Her flowered dress was adorned with a bright handkerchief pinned on her shoulder. She began the interview with:

"My dear, a miracle has happened. For seventeen years I was constipated, and for seventeen years I took a dose of mineral oil every day. This week I haven't had any mineral oil at all, and I've had perfectly normal actions—isn't that marvelous?"

I was as startled as you were the first time you realized

how important their bowels are to your counselees, but even as a first-quarter student I had learned to be noncommittal. I smiled, "Yes, Marty, it's great when all systems are go."

Marty then proceeded to tell me of a very cruel mother who had spanked her sister fifteen times in a row until she "broke her spirit." Marty was terrified of her, and the mother used Marty's terror for her own convenience. When Marty was still crawling she had developed certain phobias—one was an unreasoning fear of cotton. If mother was busy she would place cotton across the threshold of the kitchen to keep Marty out. One day in her fright and confusion Marty had a big bowel movement on the living room rug. She was beaten severely. Her mother then took her outside and tied her to a tree. Her mother then took her picture with her small face still red and swollen with crying. It was after that experience that Marty developed the case of constipation which lasted seventeen years.

The day comes when even the most accepting mother must make demands on her child. For his own future happiness he must learn some things. The most important is acceptable toilet habits. A great many things he could get by without learning and still survive in some stratum of society: he can use horrible English or have bad table manners, he can even be a crook or a parasite and still find his niche in the world, but there is one person that no civilized group I ever heard of will tolerate, and that is one who does not go to the toilet at the right time and in the right place. This he must learn, and because the mother knows he must, she often becomes anxious and starts teaching him too early for the child's own good.

"I nearly died of embarrassment," Nadine, the minister's wife, was talking to her best friend. "You know Bishop Black and his wife spent the weekend at the parsonage. Well, about eight Sunday morning I missed my three-year-old—and where do you suppose I found him? In the *bathroom* watching Mrs.

Black use the toilet! When I got there he was saying, in that grave manner of his, 'Gee—you sure use a lot of toilet paper, Mrs. Black.' "

Too often the parents try to teach a child something he has already lost interest in or is not yet emotionally ready to learn. In the matter of toilet training, some mothers try to teach their children bowel and sphincter control before their muscles develop to the point where it is even physically possible. And since the child really wants to please his mother and feels inadequate and bad if he cannot please her, it is placing quite a strain on him to insist that, in order to please her, he must accomplish the impossible. All through life such a person is apt to feel that no matter how hard he tries, he can never succeed; or to be constantly making greater and greater efforts to please without the relaxation that follows success.

One young couple asked their doctor when they should start to toilet-train their child, and the doctor said, "When your child is old enough to say, 'Mother, may I please go to the toilet?' " Of course that was just another way of saying that, given enought time and encouragement for learning, each will motivate himself and learn whatever is necessary in his own time and at his own speed. The main trouble with parents is that they want to teach their child when it suits *them;* if on the contrary, they would be alert for the time when the *child* wants to learn, all learning would be easier for both parent and child.

Many more things than constipation can be caused from too early and too severe a period of toilet training. Extremely neat and extremely dirty persons may both be reacting against faulty toilet training. Two mechanics can work on the same car: one will barely look at it before he's covered with grease from head to foot, while the other will take it apart and put it back together again without getting a spot on him. Both are reflecting their toilet training. It is the same way with housekeepers: some homes are so dirty that you have to pick your way carefully through the living room, while others are so painfully neat that you cannot be comfortable in them without fear of wrinkling a pillow or tracking in a spot of dust. Extravagance, stinginess, generosity, frigidity, impotence, and the inability to accept for himself those things which are his due—all spring from the mistakes made by the mother in this important period. Most parents have studied some psychology, and most have heard of the laws of learning; they remember the law of readiness, but unfortunately the only readiness considered is that of the parent!

Now begins an often heartbreaking struggle for power. This need not be so. If the child learns to go to the toilet because he sees the adults or older children do so it can be a happy experience and quite rewarding for both child and parent, another step in his delightful climb toward maturity. During this period the child learns that he manufactures within his own body something his mother wants. She wants him to produce this material of his at a certain time and in a certain place. If he loves his mother and feels confident of her love he has a normal desire to please her, and he will try to accede to her wishes. If on the other hand he fears her and she makes this an unpleasant experience for him, he will discover that his feces can be used as a weapon against his mother. He finds that he can infuriate her at will, simply by going at the wrong time and in the wrong place, or failing to go at the right time in the right place! Or he finds that he can embarrass his mother by waiting until company is present and then messing up the living room. Or he finds that he can cause his mother to express great pleasure and affection by doing just exactly what she asks, at just exactly the right time.

Thus, for him, his feces become a sort of currency. First you will remember that, as the child tried to understand the realities of his existence, the feces represented the mother herself, a very valuable asset in the life of any child. But now he is older and recognizes his mother as a separate person. His fantasies about the good mother and the bad mother have passed into the limbo of forgotten things. He is still aware, until a much later period in his childhood, of feelings that separate the parts of his mother's personality into two distinct people; but he is not aware, so keenly as he was, of the feeling of having eaten and ejected his mother from his bowels.

Thus, the same medium through which he once expressed his feelings for his mother now serve again to express his feelings toward her, in a different way. They become the symbol of this struggle for power, and the symbol of his ability to bargain. For the first time in his life the child discovers that he has a currency his mother wants. He may present it to her as a gracious gift, or he may withhold it as an act of defiance, but it is the first thing that the child recognizes as his own production. For the first time he has an *opportunity to decide* whether he will or will not conform to the demands of society. Up to this time he has had no language. He was turned over, warmed, fed, or dried at his mother's pleasure. Whatever was done was done for him, not by him; but now he finds there is something he makes inside his own body that his mother very much wants but cannot get unless he chooses to give it. So that in the strange world of the infant, feces become equated with money.

It takes only the slightest effort to recall such familiar expressions in our everyday language as "filthy lucre" and "squeezing the penny" to recognize the anal quality of our thinking about money, to say nothing of the fact that money itself is represented by gold, a metal that is useless, as a matter of fact, except for what it represents—namely, currency, bargaining power, buying power, and the color of an infant's warm new feces! This is the period in which the child begins to learn the demands of his society, and the struggle for his individuality as he conforms or fails to conform to these demands. It may be hard to believe that the attitude of the trustees toward giving and using money for the church is influenced still by the quality of the toilet training each received at the hands of his mother, but look around the table at the next board meeting. Many of them sit with thin lips clamped together, poised to shake their heads at some proposal they know to be forthcoming, as if they were still saying, "No, mama, I won't go."

Not only does the child learn about dirt and cleanliness at this time; he learns about giving and receiving and about buying and selling.

Just as some people cannot give, others cannot accept anything for themselves. I had a friend who had been very kind and generous to me; I had lived in her home for a week. To express my gratitude I sent her and her husband a tray. After I returned home I received this note: "We were so thrilled to receive your beautiful gift—I cannot tell you how touched at your thoughtfulness we were. But we have a tray. We do not believe in having more than we need of anything. So I took it back to the store. I told the shop-girl that you had had the pleasure of giving it and we had had the pleasure of receiving it, and that she could have it. You will find it credited to your account."

I asked a psychiatrist, "What is the matter with these people? They have been very generous *to* me, but they cannot accept any generosity *from* me."

The psychiatrist, smiling, replied, "Probably they had too much praise for going to the toilet in their early training."

It is just as important to be able to receive as it is to give. Some persons can do one, and some can do the other; some cannot do either without feeling awkward about it. If the mother does not make too much of an issue of the toilet training, both giving and receiving are accepted as a normal part of life.

Persons who retain their childhood interest in the bodily excretions often do not realize their interest in their own most private productions. Instead they are consumed with an interest in their temperature; or they show a tremendous concern over the quality and quantity of their food; or they recount at great length the details of their many illnesses, real or imaginary, or the illnesses, temperatures, stools of their children, or even of their pets! In other persons this interest has been translated into other kinds of productions. They find pleasure in doing a beautiful piece of art work. Painting of all kinds is done because the painter loves to smear; thus a childish interest in his own feces may develop in the normal person into an interest in his own or another's art. In all the phases of a child's development we shall see that these early interests have the potential of becoming quite socially acceptable in later life. To realize this gives some encouragement to the counselor who sees that for the sick, a healthy activity may be substituted using the same basic interest.

The most important way in which this period of toilet training is reflected is in the attitude toward authority, which, little as it may seem to be at first glance, is directly related to the conscience of the individual. It is normal to respond to love with love, to want to please the parents, who are the first authorities a child knows. Given enough love any child will be easy to manage; he will be sweet and amenable and friendly, and he will be sociable, acceding to the demands and frustrations imposed on him by society without too much rebellion. The natural spontaneity of the individual who responds to the demands of life without either whining or fighting springs from a healthy conscience nurtured in love from infancy. Given a chance to express his aggression and anger at home, a child develops normal, healthy relationships with others. He learns to compete without bitterness; he learns to be aggressive or not as the occasion demands; he does not have to be always belligerent or always "nice."

The most common mistakes parents make are in this area of aggression. I know parents who lay claim to a great belief in nonviolence. So important is this theory to them that if one child strikes another, the parent will beat the tar out of him to teach him the virtue of nonviolence! If they do not allow him to defend himself in a normally aggressive manner against the aggressions of his own generation of youngsters, the child may live in constant fear. Or they may demand surface politeness, sweetness, and cooperation without allowing any opportunity for the child to "blow off steam." When you find a very rebellious individual, you see one who has been heckled too much and too early about his behavior.

Psychopaths, or sociopaths as they are sometimes called, who seem to have no conscience at all are found to have been the objects of their parents' hostility from earliest infancy. They have been beaten, kicked about, shunted from one foster home to another, never having a healthy identification with an adult who would inspire the development of a conscience. You will run across many "juvenile delinquents" in your church for whom you may be the first really loving adult figure they have had the opportunity to know and from whom they may acquire a healthy conscience. This they will do, not because you tell them what is right and what is wrong, but because you accept *them* for what they are, because you love them and thus arouse the dormant gratitude from which a healthy conscience springs.

In my town some immature adolescents went into a house and tore it all apart. Before they left, they defecated on the floor and urinated on the walls. This is evidence of the fact that some of our youth have not assimilated their toilet training. Many grown people have not, as is evidenced in some of the common vulgarisms of the man on the street: "Shit on you," "Piss on you too, sister," or "Shit to hell." Just as your grown-up counselee expresses the feelings related to eating when he attempts to relate to others, so he remembers with his feelings the anguish or pleasure of his toilet training. We must help him to express hostility in a way that does not get him into trouble.

Our feelings must be expressed—indeed they will be expressed one way or another. If the God-given feeling of aggressiveness is shut off, it will find an outlet in one of the following ways:

1. In "nicey-nice" behavior, which only thinly veils the anger boiling within.

2. In overemphasis on anger to avoid showing tender or loving or hurt feelings.

3. In sneaky ways such as excessive use of alcohol or drugs.

Hostility is even expressed through sex. Remember Dr. Naylor's pregnant teen-ager? You may find some of your young members strike out at their parents by getting themselves into trouble through sex. But these topics are better discussed in the next chapter.

5
Male and Female
Created He Them

"Look Mama—two noses!" Amy exclaimed, pointing at her brother's penis, absorbed as children always are in the body and its functions. Children are particularly fascinated by their genitals—and those of others. As in the case of Amy this discovery was merely one of observation.

Early in the life of any child comes the discovery that there are two kinds of people. Some are called girls, the others are called boys. The discovery takes on the emotional tone with which the parents look upon matters of sex.

Lillian and John, a bit nearer the same age, had almost come to blows before mother arrived on the scene.

"Mother!" cried Lillian (in this case the younger of the two), tears streaming down her face. "John says I haven't got a talleywhacker. I have too got a talleywhacker, haven't I, Mother?"

In the manner of small children they forgot the presence of their mediator and turned back into the thick of the fray.

"You got no talleywhacker."

"I have too!"

"You haven't either."

"I have too!"

"You haven't either," said John, superior and supercilious. "The doctor cut it off!"

Even though the revelation of human differences surprises Lillian, her brother reacts with deeper shock. "The doctor cut it off." And thus John arrives at the conclusion reached by millions of his brothers in the human race: the girl had one once, but something happened and she lost it. We might attempt to say that uninstructed boys have this fantasy, but in actuality, like many other fantasies, it is clung to even in the face of the most careful scientific education. These home-grown explanations of the race seem to come from deep inside our feeling nature. "The doctor cut it off," or "You were bad and Father cut it off." It is regrettably true that some mothers and fathers even encourage this misconception in the little boy by threatening to "cut it off" if he masturbates. The fear of castration is as old as life itself, or almost as old. Some people think that the fear of being killed and eaten by the mother grows into the fear of castration after the child becomes aware of his genitals. The fact remains that many seemingly erratic acts on the part of children and adults stem from this childhood fear of loss. The irrational terror of the barber represents a child's unconscious fear of castration, and the boy should be treated with consideration and tenderness if he displays such fear.

With girls the situation is quite different in many ways. In this particular instance, the girl who *knows* she has always been as she is has to find another explanation for herself;

usually it consists of envy of the boy and anger at the mother. "Mother loves John more than she does me. She gave him something she wouldn't give to me!"

To many girls this handy gadget represents all the freedom that boys have and they do not have. They allow the envy to outdistance the admiration in their makeup. Such girls become man-haters; they attempt to outsmart and belittle men. These women may be very masculine or very feminine in their outward appearance, but, married or single, it is plain to the practiced eyes that their feelings toward men consist of hate, envy, and competition rather than love, admiration, and dependence. Such women are quaintly called "castrating females." They tend to marry meek men or to emotionally castrate those they do marry. The sons of such women learn to be abnormally ashamed of their genitals rather than normally proud of them. Other circumstances being unfavorable, they may develop homosexual traits just as their mothers undoubtedly have some homosexuality in their makeup.

When I had my first experience in Clinical Pastoral Education I was intrigued by the concept. One Sunday as I stood with another student in the vestibule of a church I saw a woman approach with her husband.

She was full-busted and self-confident, and she approached the church pew like a full-rigged sailing vessel attacking a strange armada. The man was several inches shorter, much thinner, and he followed along a full foot behind, taking little mincing steps. The string by which she led him was all but visible.

I whispered to my companion, "Is that what you fellows call a castrating female?" and he replied, "Yes, and from the looks of her husband, the operation has been a complete success."

Girls do not have a corner on all sexual envy. The fact that he can never have a child is distressing to many men. For a few weeks after Tim was born Buzzie watched with fascination while he was fed—he called the mother's breasts her feeding stations. Soon the mother noticed Buzzie peering earnestly at his naked body in the mirror.

"What are you doing, Buzzie?" she asked.

"I'm looking to see if my feeding stations have begun to grow," he replied.

Then it became the task of his mother to explain that he, alas, would never have feeding stations, but would grow up to be a great big man like daddy. As best he may, the child adjusts to this new disappointment; he takes on the stride and mien of his father and thus soon forgets his envy of his mother. But that he never really forgets is evident in attitudes and behavior throughout life.

As the public becomes better educated in the ways of handling this delicate and often misunderstood problem of difference between the sexes it becomes less and less necessary for the discovery of these differences to come as a shock to the individual. Better preparation of parents for child care has produced a generation of boys and girls from whom much of the "innocence" has departed, but who have replaced that so-called innocence of childhood with the intelligence and emotional balance of maturity. Most of these young people have been brought up in families where the human body is no mystery, and they are not therefore faced with a shocking discovery in the field of anatomy at the precise time in their lives when sex is becoming significant to them. However, it is doubtful that such well-brought-up persons will find their way into your office for counseling.

Sharon laughed, "My youngest said, 'You know, Daddy, I've got a ball on my bottom and it feels good when I play with it,' and Eric just smiled and said, 'Yes, doesn't it, son.' Why, in my family we'd have been skinned alive!"

In Eric's family one end of a human being is as acceptable as the other end. They are both ends of the same human being, and both are very necessary. Without either, the person cannot survive. Let us remember the words of Paul:

> "For as the body is one, and hath many members, and all the members of that one body, being many, are one body: so also is Christ. . . . For the body is not one member, but many. If the foot shall say, Because I am not the hand, I am not of the body; is it therefore not of the body? . . . If the whole body were an eye, where were the hearing? If the whole were hearing, where were the smelling? But now God hath set the members every one of them in the body. . . . And the eye cannot say to the hand, I have no need of thee. . . . Nay, much more those members of the body, which seem to be more feeble, are necessary: And those members of the body, which we think to be less honourable, upon these we bestow more abundant honour; and our uncomely parts have no need: but God hath tempered the body together, having given more abundant honor to that part which lacked: That there should be no schism in the body; but that the members should have the same care one for another." (I Corinthians 12:12-25.)

The normal pride a boy feels about his penis is sometimes damaged by parents who cannot enjoy with him feelings about his whole body.

Tommie is just ten months old. He and Mommie are playing a game called "Find me."

She says, "Hands."

He holds out his hands.

She chuckles and says, "Eyes."

He touches his eyes, and she shouts with glee.

She says, "Nose."

And when he touches his nose she says, "Good baby!"

Then he takes off on his own. He reaches down and finds his penis.

Suddenly mama scowls, spanks his hands.

"Naughty boy, Tommie. Nasty—musn't touch." The game

is over. Tommie is hurt and bewildered, and well he may be. Immediately he forms a conclusion in that little world of his own where verbal explanations have had no opportunity to penetrate because he has not learned to talk or understand explanations: "There is something the matter with me. Part of me my mother doesn't like."

What a sad situation! Tommie has no way of knowing what his own mother does not know, i.e., that his penis is fine, and for him to discover it is just as natural and right as for him to discover his eyes; that indeed the only reason his mother spanks his hands is that *her* mother spanked *her* hands, because *her* mother spanked *her* hands, because *her* mother spanked *her* hands, and that all are responding to the same irrational, unreasoning fear that serves now to confuse him.

Later another cruel awakening will befall Tommie when he discovers that his mother loves another fellow, and if he is lucky she loves this man even *better* than she loves him! It is a cruel world! The little boy receives this blow with a great deal of hostility. He is very angry at his father, he hates his father, his jealousy amounts to a murderous rage. Indeed he violently wishes his father out of the way, and to an infant or a small child this wish to have someone "out of the way" amounts to murder.

He still is confused about the meaning of death, but he remembers that when G'Mama left he asked, "Where's G'Mama now?"

Daddy said, "Heaven."

"What's heaven?"

"A pretty place where she is much happier, and where we'll all go someday."

One of these days soon Tommie will startle his father with, "Daddy, why don't you go to heaven with G'Mama so you can be happier? Mommie and I will come later."

Remember that when he nursed his mother and she went

away about her duties the child felt that he had killed her and eaten her? In an infant's thinking, "to go away" means to have been killed and eaten. He wants his father to go away; to the child this means that he would like to kill and eat his father, and he learns to fear his own feelings. The infant who would like to chew up the breast believes that it would like to chew him up too. Now Tommie believes that since he would like to kill and eat his father, his father would like to kill and eat him too.

A less awesome fear eventually takes the place of the fear that father may kill the boy—the fear that his father may merely castrate him. So the child who first experienced fears of being annihilated in his relationship to his mother on the feeding level will again experience it in relationship to his father on the sexual level.

The desire to get rid of the father is thought of in the same way as was eating up the mother at an earlier time in the child's history.

"If I want to kill Daddy he must want to kill me; and he can because he's bigger, though I can't because I'm small."

To be sure, such thoughts are not so clearly defined as a rule, but the boy's attitude toward the father becomes one of fear, envy, and hostility combined. He fiercely loves his mother and he takes every opportunity to express distaste for his father. At such a time it is not unusual for a little boy just to walk up and start kicking his father's shins without obvious provocation, or to double up his small fist and hit the unsuspecting father in the stomach, or at the least to make a few nasty remarks.

A Negro minister of my acquaintance smiled at the tack his son took to express his hostility when he said in a loud voice to his mother in the hearing of his father, "Mother, why didn't you marry a *white* man?"

Boys devise means of torturing their fathers during this stage of development, as seen in the above illustration, and the emotional future of the child at this point depends very much upon the response of the father. If the father is understanding and tolerant, and does not let the child annoy him too much but by playing rough with him and not moving away from the mother when the child demands it, shows the boy that indeed "Daddy is here to stay," he can at the same time alleviate the fears of the little boy. Children fear their unmanageable feelings and need the help of an older person to bring them into focus with reality.

It is a little extreme to say the boy "falls in love" with his mother or that the girl "falls in love" with her father, but it is foolish not to recognize that there is a strong attraction between the sexes whatever the age or relationship of the persons involved. In the Greek drama *Oedipus Rex* by Aeschylus, Oedipus is abandoned by his own parents who are the king and queen of the city-state. Reared by foster parents, he never suspects his true origin; but when he grows up he sets out for the city. He meets and takes an instant dislike to his father, the king, and kills him; subsequently he is attracted to and marries his own mother.

Here again, as in the case of Hansel and Gretel, we find an illustration of the fact that the shadows of our childhood haunt the wings of our adult theaters.

The natural solution that comes to the little boy is that he eventually finds it impossible to evict his father from the household; his daddy is indeed here to stay. He decides to make the best of it, to renounce his desire to possess his mother, and become as much like his father as it is possible for him to become.

Pete was a small Jewish boy who called himself my boyfriend. I used to go along with his idea by sending him birthday cards with the caption, "To my boyfriend." His mother told me, "You would have died laughing at Pete. When we went back home on a visit one of the relatives asked him if he had a girlfriend, and he replied gravely, "Well as a matter of fact I've got two girlfriends—I've got Louise and I've got Deborah. Now I like Louise, I like her quite a lot, but she's a good bit older than me, and by the time I get old enough to get married she's going to be even *older*. Then there's Deborah—she is almost exactly my age, and she goes to my Sunday school because she's Jewish and I'm Jewish too, which Louise isn't, so I think probably Deborah is really best for me!" Thus we see that this young man of six, who had already progressed (as most boys do) from an interest in his mother to another older woman, gradually reasons that even she is impractical for him, and he is now ready to turn to a girl his own age.

As he becomes reconciled to his position in the family you see the boy begin to walk like his father, hold his head like him, and in many ways imitate his mannerisms. In like manner the girl realizes that her mother is too much of a fixture to be got rid of. She abandons hope for possession of her father's undivided attention and becomes identified with her mother. She learns to keep house like her mother, to sing at her tasks as her mother does, to make bread like her mother. It is very amusing to watch a little girl at play with her dolls, because that is one sure way of finding out how the mother handles the children. If the child screams at her dolls, turns them across her knee, and beats the saw-dust out of them, it is easy to see in every inflection the voice and spirit of the mother. On the other hand, if she cuddles, loves, and cares for her dolls in a tender manner it is easy to see here reflected the kindly, loving mother who can be observed in the attitude of her child.

But scraps of hostility for the parent of the same sex remain, though at a later time this hostility is more easily resolved:

Mother had refused more coke and cookies. Listening at the window, she heard this:

Jane: "Let's kill her!"

John: "Let's kill them both." (Father is a strictly innocent party, being off in the city at his office.)

Jane: (Warming to her grisly little idea) "And we'll bury them in the ground!"

John: "But—if we do that, who'll give us money to buy cokes?"

Jane: "Jesus will!"

John: "Aw, Jesus is dead!"

Jane: "He is not! He lives around here somewhere in a tree."

Their theology is slightly faulty, but the solution of their conflicts is strictly on schedule. The girl, who is younger, is for killing the mother, the boy is for throwing father in for good measure, but, being older and almost out of this period, he pauses to think, "Who will give us money to buy cokes?" Probably in the back of his head: "Who will take me fishing? Who will ride me piggy-back to bed? Who will fix my bike?" Very practical, these six-year-olds.

Once their conflicts are resolved children turn with trust toward their parents for information. Sex questions can come upon an unsuspecting parent from the most innocent of beginnings.

"Daddy," grave blue eyes smile into twinkling blue eyes. "Does your belly button grow inside or outside?"

"Well, son, my belly button grows pretty much the way yours does. Why?"

"I was looking at Grandma, and hers grows in a big poop on the outside."

"Oh."

"Daddy?"

"Yes, son."

"Why does hers grow in a big poop outside?"

"It depends on the doctor you have."

"It does?"

Ralph, Sr. realized now he was trapped, so he settled down

and began: "Everyone has a belly button because the cord has to be cut, and the way the cut heals determines the way the belly button grows."

"What cord?"

"I was afraid you'd ask that. Every little baby when he's inside his mother gets his food from her through a tube called a cord."

"Does the doctor fasten the cord to Mommie?"

"No, it grows there."

"How did I ever get in there?"

"I put you in."

"Didn't it hurt Mommie?"

Ralph silently crossed his fingers. "No. She had fun."

"When you put *me* in *her*?"

"Well, you were quite small then."

"Why did you put me there?"

(Warming to his subject) "Actually, I didn't. I just put my half in. She was saving her half inside her, waiting all those years for me to bring her my half of you."

"Suppose someone else had put their half in there with Mommie's half of me?"

"You wouldn't be you."

"Gee—Dad, can we talk some more later, I have to go now."

"Great, son, great. You just go right ahead."

Children often feel the threat of too much knowledge just as we do, and they need time to absorb new information.

Sometime near age eleven, just before the beginning of puberty, all boys and girls try masturbating. Masturbation is a universal practice which begins usually about the end of the second year, persists awhile, halts, starts up just before the advent of puberty (perhaps it is actually the beginning of puberty) and stops again with the onset of adolescence. This is the normal course of the practice, but many, many opportunities for error beset this particular bit of the child's development. Sexual intercourse is normal for adults, and usually something is wrong at home when a grown man or woman masturbates regularly; but the development of the child, male or female, invariably includes a certain amount of masturbation, and there is nothing wrong with him when he does it. Many persons look on this childhood pleasure with undue alarm. It has been proved many times that this activity is indeed harmless, yet you will find persons who believe that it will cause insanity, cancer, syphilis, pregnancy, baldness, and goodness knows what all! Most persons seeking counseling have been told some of these old wives' tales somewhere along the line, and they feel guilty about it. If we ourselves are able to listen to their confession, they will tell us, receive our reassurance, and feel an untold relief.

Many men have been taught to fear the loss of semen as a result of masturbation. Too few have fathers like my little friend, Pete, who said, "But, Daddy, in going to the bathroom or something [by "something" his father knew Pete referred to his little bedtime games] suppose I should lose some of those little baby seeds—what would happen then?"

"Well, son," said the wise father, "we have so many thousands of baby seeds that if we should lose a few there's no harm done."

Many things can happen to interfere with the normal development of the child: the mother or the father may not understand or take kindly to the child's opposition; the interest of the child in sex may be thought to be "abnormal" at so tender an age and may be beaten down (sometimes literally) by parents with the most righteous intent. The mother or father may die, there may be separation or divorce, there may be the interference of in-laws, a young brother or sister may arrive at exactly the wrong time. War may take away the father for a time or even forever. Among all the multifarious possibilities for error your counselee is sure to have encoun-

tered one or more, or he would not be here today sitting in
your office chair looking miserable.

Many problems will be brought to the counselor disguised
as problems of theology because the members of the congregation fear a shocked reaction to their talking about sex.
Most ministers today are more broad-minded than their members realize, but this fact is unknown to the average counselee,
who expects the minister to be moralistic and condemnatory.
It will be his good fortune and the counselor's skill which
will give him leeway to talk about any and all things that
are in his mind.

The ladies' magazines talk delicately about what can save
a marriage, about what most frequently mentioned problems
plague a marriage—like money, in-laws, religious differences
—but I have found that a couple who is happy together in
bed is happy all the way, and all the other problems, real
though they may be, are minor matters by comparison.

One of my favorite avenues into the real marriage difficulties of the persons I counsel is to say, "How did you two
happen to get married in the first place?" Often as not the
sad end of the marriage was incipient in its beginning, and
I get some unusual responses to this seemingly innocent
question.

Like Jane: "Because *my mother* was so in love with him
I married him to shut her up."

Or Ted: "Well, all the other GI's were getting married,
and she was pushing it so I did."

Or Marian: "I couldn't stand to see my sister married
before I was, so I ran away the weekend before her wedding
and I beat her to the altar, but she's having a baby before
I do anyway and it's killing me."

Or Sally: "I don't know what Dan thinks," she said of
her husband. "I don't understand him very well. We aren't
as close as people think we are."

"How did you happen to marry Dan?"

"I had to."

"How do you mean that?"

"I had to."

"You mean you were pregnant?"

"Yes. And my mother found it out on my wedding day." She burst into violent weeping.

"How did she take it?"

"She had a fit. So that the day that should have been my happiest was . . ." She broke off and sobbed. When she became calm I asked,

"How did your mother find it out?"

"I got sick at my wedding dinner and had to go to the bathroom. As I was leaving the table *Dan's mother* turned to her and said, 'Isn't it too bad? She's starting to be sick already.' "

"How did *she* know?"

"Oh, Dan *told his* mother."

"How did you meet Dan?"

"We worked at the same place. I adored him. He would notice me only when he felt like it. He went out with other girls whenever he wanted. I would keep back my resentment and smile at him the next day. No matter how he ignored me I would always make some advance, I was so crazy about him. I 'got my man'—and lived to regret it" (bitterly).

Many times Sally has said, "There's just one thing I want —*my freedom!*" But she always adds, "I can't separate my children or deprive them of a home."

Once she said, "Oh, I felt so terrible Saturday night. You know I told you Dan has been teaching me to drive? Well, last Saturday night he wanted to take his mother riding, and he suggested I drive. I didn't do it to suit him. When we got home both of them jumped on me and told me what an awful driver I was. She said I made living twice as expensive for her Danny. I went to my room and cried for hours. I don't know *when* I've cried so!"

"Did you tell them how *you* felt about *them?*"

"No."

"Why not?"

"I wanted to keep the peace."

"Have you peace?"

"Oh—well."

A few hints have been dropped as to how problems develop regarding homosexuality, masturbation, infidelity, envy of the position of the male in our society by the female, fear of castration on the part of the male. But let us now take a closer look.

Among other ways of solving their little problem of identity in the family, children turn to one another for companionship. At age six and seven they explore one another's anatomy. You know and I know it is quite normal, harmless, and right on schedule, but parents make many blunders at this point.

Like Ada, who said, looking desperate, "I know it's all right for Jimmie to be interested in little girls, but when Julie's mother called me to come and get him she had already spanked Julie and she told me I should spank him. She had found them under the house with their pants off. I was so embarrassed and upset and mad with Julie's mother that I turned Jimmie across my knee and really beat him with a coat hanger. I feel awful. What can I do?"

"Have you thought of apologizing to him? Of explaining that you were, as you said, embarrassed and upset and mad at Julie's mother and you took it out on him?"

"No, but I'll try it."

The next day she was back:

"Children are so wonderful. Jimmie forgave me and put his arms around me and then he said, 'You know, Mama, when you were hitting me you looked awful—like you were mad at Jesus and God and everybody.'"

Some incidents do not turn out so happily. Incidents like

the above could cause the child to be fearful or hostile to the opposite sex, and even to turn to homosexuality.

Gene sat looking at me with big owl eyes. "I have a terrible problem. I'm a homosexual."

"How do you know?"

"Well, when I was twelve and thirteen, along in there, I used to go and spend the night with my friend and we'd play with each other. Then the other night I took my girl out and I felt cold when I kissed her."

"What's your girl like?" (Don't jump on his "homosexuality" right away; aerate his information.)

"Oh, she's not much of a girl really. She's got funny teeth and she's wearing braces, but she's the best I could get."

"So maybe you wouldn't have wanted to kiss her even if you hadn't played with your friend."

"Hey" (laughing), "you could be right."

"What did you mean when you said, 'She's the best I could get'?"

"I'm not very popular with the good-looking ones" (wistfully).

"No?"

"No—I'm afraid they're smart and maybe they know something is wrong with me."

"What's wrong with you?"

"Well, you know, like I told you about my problem of homosexuality."

"Is your problem homosexuality, or is it that you think there is something wrong with you?"

"There is more wrong with me than you know." Tears come, quickly dashed away with a cuff.

"Don't mind me. Cry if you feel like it."

"I'm not crying."

"Well, if you should feel like it sometime, don't mind me."

"I told my dad, 'I hate you—I wish you were dead.' Next week he was killed in a wreck." He breaks into uncontrollable sobbing. So he was right—there is more wrong with him, and his unrealistic condemnation of himself comes from deep inside his aching heart. Many tears and years later he finds a way to love a girl who truly loves him in return.

Many youngsters without the helpful understanding of a knowledgeable adult may get hooked on homosexuality, but if they are helped at an early enough age, the counselor or parent may uncover the self-hate that is a large part of every homosexual's makeup and enable him to find a full sexual life after all.

People sometimes wander into homosexuality by accident or ignorance. Unfortunately, homosexuality is often encouraged by the most righteous of parents, by indirection. It is even encouraged by the church! Yes, it is! So much stress is placed on the evils of heterosexuality, the dangers of unwanted pregnancy, and the dangers of masturbation, that little or no mention is made of homosexuality (its being considered quite beneath the pale). Then a boy or a girl may be well into the practice before he knows what is happening. He may feel vaguely guilty without a true knowledge of his condition. I have known seminary students who were married and had children before they became aware that they had homosexual tendencies.

Usually homosexuality is developed in a home where the parent of the same sex is domineering and the parent of the opposite sex does not rescue the child from this domination. It even happens when the opposite is true, i.e., when the parent of the opposite sex is the domineering one and the parent of the same sex is unwilling or unable to come to the rescue. Given such fruitful soil the child often falls into the hands of an older practicing homosexual and thus establishes a pattern of overt homosexual behavior. More often children are not exposed to the practice of homosexual play, and their tendencies remain unconscious. Sometimes these tendencies take the form of so-called Don Juanism, in which a man flits from girl to girl all his life trying desperately to prove to himself that he is a man. In women it may take the form of promiscuity, or, combined with a very practical turn of mind, this defect is sometimes turned to rather lucrative account in the old, if not honored, profession of prostitution.

No matter what the symptom, there is one thing a counselor dare not forget: his counselee is suffering, and suffering to the point of being willing to do something positive about it. He is here for help, not for a lecture on morals. No doubt he knows the moral code as well as you do. If he could keep it he would. If we are to help these helpless individuals who come to us crippled emotionally then we must keep alive that compassion with which Jesus looked on the crippled ones who came to him. In no instance did the Master grasp the occasion to read his followers a lecture on the moral code. To *no one*—not to the woman at the well, not to Zacchaeus, not to the woman taken in adultery, not to Mary Magdalene —did he speak a word of criticism. One and all, he treated them for what they were—emotionally sick people in need of his help.

The counselee suffers. He doesn't know what he suffers from, but many times a discussion of what seemed at first to be a sexual problem reveals a problem of hostility.

The boy Gene, who thought he was a homosexual, was really in misery over his father's death and his own confused feelings of love and hate.

In our present culture, though the sexual revolution is far from over and many counselees have sexual problems, the deepest and most unresolved difficulties are those relating to anger in all its forms. In the next chapter we shall see how growing up involves both sex and anger and thus makes it natural to confuse the two.

6

If a Man Hate Not His Mother and Father

"If anyone comes to me and does not hate his father and mother and wife and children and brothers and sisters, aye and his own life, he cannot be a disciple of mine" (Luke 14:26 Moffatt).

Jesus expected maturity of his followers. He knew that no man who is tied to his mother's (or father's) apron strings is going to be a leader of men, and so, in his dramatic way, he made the point with which this chapter opens. The proper time for a child to "hate his mother and father" is the no-man's-land that begins with puberty and ends with adulthood.

Bodily changes take place which make the child's interest in sex suddenly flare up. In addition he needs to begin thinking of getting out on his own and earning a living; he becomes acutely aware of his competition with the parent of the same sex. Such things are frightening especially if a person has been held down and made to feel dependent for the first ten or twelve years of his life, and it is not easy for him to break away. The parents also are greatly distressed by the changed attitudes on the part of their erstwhile docile offspring. He insists on having his own way, he calls his parents squares, he defies his father, he laughs at his mother, he lets his hair grow. The more anxious he is the more likely he is to come into conflict with authority, whether in the school or on the city streets. It is suddenly as if a new person entered the household in the form of this familiar looking individual.

Even parents who have been relatively relaxed in the handling of their children up to this point find themselves frustrated, infuriated, and confounded by this half-man, half-beast we call the adolescent. He wants to act like a child and yet be treated like a man. The parent wants to continue to treat him like a child but expects him to behave like a grown-up. This conflict between the generations causes many bitter recriminations and many salty tears in the households of our land.

I think there is only one teen-ager in my town. No matter who his parents are they always say the same things: "He won't mow the grass—won't mow unless paid—does a lousy job of mowing—leaves tools out after mowing—tracks in grass clippings—talks back—goes out with girls." Or, "She keeps a filthy room—won't keep her room—keeps animals of all kinds in her room—won't wash dishes—won't iron her own clothes—talks back—goes out with boys."

Sometimes I tease parents a little with the questions:
"Is your child failing in classes?"
"No."
"Stealing hubcaps?"
"No!"
"Taking LSD?"

"No!!"

"Selling drugs?"

"No!!"

"Pregnant?"

"Oh, no!!"

Then I shrug, "You're doing all right." Sometimes it helps them see their child as a normal teen-ager. Sometimes it makes them angry. Either way it leads to further discussion.

The advice that works best with parents if they would follow it is: "Get off the kid's back."

I will always remember a robin I watched many springs ago. I was a student, and a patient of mine was with me. We sat in the hospital garden watching Mama Robin push Junior out of the nest. He was squawking and resisting as she pushed.

"You silly bird," my little companion said. "You'd better be glad your mother is helping you to get out of that nest and fly on your own; else at age thirty-five you might be like me, having to consult Miss Long."

Teen-agers try to cut apron strings. We would be better off to help them, but many adults try instead to hinder. Parents who have treasured their authority in earlier years find it hard to relinquish, but some are smart.

Remember Norma? When her first was born her doctor gave her a schedule of feeding. She was a bit in advance of her time and had been reading all the latest baby books, so she informed him, "I plan to feed my baby on demand: when he's hungry he'll let me know and I'll feed him. I'll feed that baby just as much as he wants and as often as he wants and no more."

The doctor was furious. "If you do that you are on your own!"

"All right, Doctor, I'm on my own."

At age six weeks the baby had worked himself into a schedule of feeding approximately every four hours. He slept all through the night and was sweet and content, a joy to all who knew him. Norma's friends were saying, "Norma, you are so lucky; you have a good baby." And Norma was saying back, "Lucky, huh!"

Cutting the apron strings begins in the cradle. When a child is ready to go to school we think of his education as having begun. As a matter of fact, the most important part of his education is finished. Whatever is built thereupon is mere superstructure. Safely through the three most dramatic periods of childhood, our boy or girl has already formed ideas about his place in the world—he feels accepted or he feels that no one wants to be bothered with him; he has his own ideas about sex—either he takes it as a natural part of life or he feels it is something dirty to be shunned and hidden; he is able to handle his hostilities within the family pretty well, and whatever sadistic feelings he has he takes out on children his age or younger behind the backs of any disapproving adults. He laughs; he plays; if he fights it is with his contemporaries. In the schoolroom and at home he is relatively cooperative and sociable. He seems to take no interest in members of the opposite sex. He eats, sleeps, and goes to the toilet as a matter of course. If he is a boy there is usually a problem of cleanliness; seldom is this true if she is a girl.

During the intensive period of socialization which has taken place for the first few years of his life the child has learned to repress or suppress many of the feelings that he has at this time. But this halcyon time—this honeymoon of childhood—is short-lived, as are all phases of development. Soon it gives place to the stormy years known as adolescence.

Pete, glowing with his newfound manhood, announced, "Mother, I belong to the *Hate Girl* club now." Very soon, long before we think of the child as having entered puberty, he begins to torture the little girls in preference to torturing the little boys in the schoolroom. He pulls their ponytails, he smears jam on their white dresses, he puts cockleburs in their hair, he steals their books, and he maintains he has no interest in, and certainly no affection for, these sissy little creatures whom he finds it impossible to let alone. He refuses to kiss or be kissed. If he walks down the street with his mother he pretends not to be with her or know who she is. This period marks the reawakening of his sexual feeling, even though he expresses it in a very negative manner.

During this age it is quite normal for boys to be extremely fond of boys their own age and for girls to be extremely fond of girls. It is the time for normal homosexual relationships, which will, in turn, give way to normal heterosexual relationships if undisturbed by conflicts carried over from a younger age.

Some parents can take adolescence in their stride. I shall never forget Dr. Jones, a father whom I learned to respect more than any other parent I had ever seen in action. His son, fourteen, was going out on a date, and he made the announcement, "And on this date I am taking Cubby." Now, Cubby was the family dog, very low slung, very hairy, rather smelly, quite doggy: there was really nothing about Cubby that was appropriate for a date that the young man might have with his girl friend. And so this father said to his son, "Oh, no! I certainly would *not* take *Cubby*." The son, now halfway up the stairs, leaned over the banisters, looked his father in the eye, and said with care, precision, and firmness, "*I am taking Cubby*." To my astonishment, the father shrugged his shoulders, turned away, and said not another word—and Cubby went on the date!

It was the first contact I had had with the Jones family, and later contacts were to prove as astonishing—that is, if one expects all children to speak with deference to parents and hop at their command. This father maintained that a son of fourteen was able to drive a car, manage his own life, and make his own decisions. There were many storms in that family, some of them likely to end in disaster for child or parent, but at no time was the disaster a disaster to human personality. Every child in that family was allowed and expected to make his own decisions about the major issues of his life: whom he would love; what he would wear; when he would come in at night; what he would expect of himself; where, when, and even if, he would go to college; the choice of his profession; the choice of his life mate. All these things were matters for the individual to decide, and the father would take no part in making the decisions for the children. At the same time, he restrained his wife, who would have been much more eager (so she says) to tell her growing children what their role in life should be. After they were all grown up and settled, Matilda Jones said to me one day, "It's all to the credit of my husband. I would have told them what to do, but he wouldn't let me."

An older son called long distance one night late in August. Matilda came out on the porch saying indignantly to her husband, "Morris—that's little Morris! [Little Morris was twenty-one.] And he wants to skip this term of college and go to Europe on a freighter. You go talk to him and tell him he can't go; tell him he's got to finish college."

"Why Mattie," said "big" Morris mildly, "I can't do that. He'll have to make up his own mind, but I'll be glad to talk to him of course."

He walked into the house, talked a few minutes on the phone, and came back.

"What did he say?" asked his mother.

"Said he'd see us at Christmas," replied her husband laconically.

"Little Morris" did see them at Christmas and returned happily enough to college. He remained for a graduate degree and became a minister as his father had been before him.

A boy whose father treats him with some respect in the

early years can afford to identify with him when he grows up, being neither too frightened nor too rebellious to compete with the old man.

The Jones family is a rare household, the like of which this country could stand many more. In it no one hated mother or father for long because hate was made unnecessary. Unfortunately, many men and women *must* hate their mothers and fathers in order to gain the independence so freely given by the Joneses. The warmth and the love with which the adults look now on their aging parents bring joy to the hearts of those who knew the struggles through which the parents went as they exercised the only thing really necessary in the rearing of an adolescent—namely, self-control.

The counselee may gnash his teeth in resentment as he remembers the restrictions of his adolescence. He may flout authority in the face because, at the time when it was normal and right for him to do so in order to gain his independence, he was forced to remain tied to his mother's apron strings.

"I think God knew what he was doing when he made teen-agers," said Ellen. "Because by the time they are ready to leave home they have become so obnoxious we're really glad to see them go." Funny girl, Ellen, but the truth is that God didn't make teen-agers. We did.

Until a little over a hundred years ago, in America, young people were married at the age of fifteen or sixteen, some even at the ages of thirteen and fourteen. Adolescence was unknown. In the pioneer days a boy of fifteen could cut down a tree about as well as, or even better than, a man of fifty. The young man of eighteen could go to war (and still does) with better chances of survival than the man of thirty-five. His judgment may not be so good, but his aim is more sure because his eyesight is apt to be better. In the simpler civilizations, men are men at fifteen or sixteen, and up, and women are women much younger. A girl of twelve can bear a baby and take care of him in the way she takes care of a doll, if she does not at the same time have to be earning a Ph.D., teaching school, and putting her husband through seminary! In our present age we throw up our hands in holy horror at the thought of "children" marrying at so tender an age. "They just aren't able to handle the responsibilities of marriage," we say. They are quite as able to handle the responsibilities of *marriage* as they have always been in previous centuries, but they are *not* able to handle the demands of the highly trained professions. And so we have with us a new creature—the adolescent—an individual who is, in his own mind, a grown-up; in the minds of his parents, a child. He is economically dependent, so he cannot fulfill his sexual desires, which are at the full term. His economic dependence warps and angers him. Good parents can make the life of an adolescent one of relative pleasure. Or shall we, perhaps, say reduce the hell through which an adolescent inevitably goes. Maturity can be achieved more rapidly with help from the parents; even so, breaking away from the pleasures of dependence is never an unmixed blessing. There are fathers and mothers who cannot bear to part from their adolescent children.

Al was a young minister who understood people. Janice Stone, sixteen, was crying, "My dad won't let me go out with Stan. He said I was never to let him catch Stan hanging around the house. But I love Stan—I *can't* quit seeing him. I've been meeting him at the pizza parlor Saturday afternoons when I know Dad is playing golf. But now it's time for the senior prom, and Stan wants to pick me up at home."

"Well, why don't you let him?"

"Dad would *kill* him!"

"Maybe not."

"Sometimes I think Dad is actually jealous of Stan, and then I feel so ashamed for thinking such a thing."

"You could be right. Many a parent is jealous of his own child—or of her boyfriends."

"Sometimes I think Mama is jealous of me."

"Maybe."

"Dad and I always got along better than he and Mama did until Stan came along. Oh, Al, what shall I do?"

"Why don't you try letting Stan come to the house? Your dad can't take you to the prom."

"O.K. I'll try, but don't be surprised if you get an emergency call."

Three days later that is exactly what happened. Al was just sitting down to his dinner when the phone rang and Janice, crying hysterically, pleaded, "Oh, Al, please come right away—I'm afraid Dad and Stan are going to kill each other."

Al hastened to the Stone home where he found Mike Stone, chairman of the church board and as level-headed a man at a board meeting as he'd ever seen, standing in the middle of the living room floor squared off to Stan, captain of the high school football team. To Al it seemed that mayhem was indeed imminent. The boy and his future father-in-law were facing each other like a couple of strange tomcats. Janice and her mother were in tears. Unbidden and certainly unwelcome at such a moment came a clear memory of the check old man Stone wrote out for the church every month. It was hard to recognize the situation as an opportunity, but no one in the room would have suspected the turmoil in Al's heart when they heard his quiet, "Cool it, you cats."

Stone looked a little sheepish, and Stan relaxed a mite. Al sat down on the couch and crossed his legs, exuding a moral courage he did not feel.

Stone stammered, red-faced, "He's trying to take her out."

"Yes."

"Yes he is."

"To the high school prom?"

"Yes. How did *you* know?" (suspiciously).

"Everybody in town knows tonight's the annual prom.

Every kid in town will be there and every teacher too. Many parents go."

Silence. Silence. Silence. At last Stone said, "You kids get out of here. I want to talk to the preacher."

The two young people fled. Stone turned on Al, "This is your doing. All your talk of freedom and self-determination. I'll cut that contribution of mine to the bone. You'll see."

"I'm sorry you ever got the impression, Stoney, that you could buy my conscience."

"What?!"

"Let me put it this way. I appreciate your interest in the church, but I thought the check was for God's work. I'd no idea you thought you were controlling me with it."

"Oh, please." For the first time Mrs. Stone spoke. "Don't fight the preacher."

"Nobody's fighting. Shut up, Stella."

"No, please, Stoney—let's hear from her. How does it look to you, Stella?"

"He's just nuts about that girl—"

(Interrupting) "Your daughter?"

"Yes—Janice. *His* daughter from the day she was born—you'd think she only had one parent."

"Now, Stella—"

"Don't 'Now Stella' me—it's abnormal, that's what it is." She wept.

"Is it normal for a man to want to protect his child from some lecherous kid twice her size?" (Yelling.) "Why if he tried to rape her, she wouldn't have a chance!"

"You think he wants to rape her, Stoney?"

"Don't they all—this undisciplined younger generation?"

"Do you want to, Stoney?"

Dead silence.

"What are you accusing me of, *Reverend?*" (Clinching and unclinching his fist.)

"Come on, Stoney, in the privacy of your own heart,

haven't you ever thought about any of those pretty little teen-agers in the Sunday school?"

Stoney's face reddened, and tears filled his eyes. "Preacher, you're a mind reader—you're a devil."

"No, Stoney, I just know men. I'm one myself, remember?"

Stoney, weeping openly now, said, "How can I be like that toward my own daughter? It's your fault" (turning on Stella).

"*Mine?* What have I ever done?"

"Nothing—that's what—nothing. I loved you and I've longed for you, but you were so jealous of Janice that you couldn't even love me anymore."

"*You* couldn't love *me* anymore. From the moment you saw her I didn't exist for you."

"Oh, Stella—you're my *wife*—I *love* you."

"You don't show it."

Al spoke up, "Perhaps if you both try showing it a little more you won't have time to be so wrapped up in Janice's love life."

The one-in-a-million minister or youth leader like Al who can successfully hold joint meetings of teen-agers and parents is a real artist. Most of us can hold group discussions with the adolescents in the church, and separate meetings with their parents. It is a brave man who can bring them together, either by families or in larger groups.

One minister, a man locally rather famous for his program of Christian education, used to say, "The best time to reach parents is when the first child hits adolescence. They are so frustrated and filled with guilt because they think they're failures as parents that you can nab them and teach them a few things."

Had he been aware of his opportunities earlier, Al could have avoided his near tragic predicament by foreseeing it. Parents' classes are usually welcomed more by the parents of teen-agers who have begun to feel the pinch, but it is the younger siblings who profit more in the long run than the teen-agers themselves.

An approach to the problems of the family that takes in each individual as well as the total group is best. The following chart is sometimes helpful in handling the problems of whole families:

	father	mother	daughter (son)	boyfriend (girl-)	sibling	sibling
emotional needs						
immediate problem						
possibili- ties of solution						
plan of approach						

113

After filling all blanks for each individual involved in the situation, check back: how many of the possible solutions are in conflict with one another? How may you approach this whole situation in order to minimize the conflicts and still maintain the greatest good for the greatest number? You should have a chart on every family in your congregation, so you can check periodically how the situation has changed and what methods have brought about the changes.

Often problems of adolescents reveal the problems of their parents: A neighbor said, "Georgia Drake is only twelve years old, yet she is the most marvelous help I ever saw. I hope my child will turn out to be just half the help to me that she is to her mother." Yet I had observed other characteristics in the girl. She has an overeager manner with adults; she talks too rapidly and too enthusiastically as if it were necessary to say everything before the adult gets away again. She often exhibits the same manner with children her own age and is promptly repulsed. Both her mother and her father speak with unnecessary sharpness when addressing her, and both expect of her a maturity beyond her years.

Mary, her mother, explained this situation to me once quite unexpectedly: "I never forgave Georgia for being the cause of my marrying George. I know it's a terrible way to be, but I can't help it. Oh, we get along better now than we used to. Since we have lived here he hasn't been as bad about running around with other women. He was always getting into trouble when he used to be on the road more. Two summers ago my sister begged me to leave him. But I hang on for the children's sake. He's better now, but he still comes in from trips talking about the dames he's met and the old girl friends he took to dinner while I've been home working."

Just as the problems of children reveal parents' problems, so problems of husbands lead into the problems of their wives and vice versa. In the midst of all these crosscurrents stands the minister, attempting to be the friend of all. This is no easy task, and if he fails he knows that the original family problem may eventually disguise itself as a full-fledged church war. Many an inherited schism in the church can be traced back to what originally started as an argument between sisters or in-laws! Hence the family approach to this problem may save not only the immediate family but the whole church as well.

Because adolescence is the period when most youngsters attempt to break away from their domineering parents, it seems to be the one most fraught with difficulty. Many juvenile delinquents begin their careers at this time. Delinquency is nothing more than a neurotic symptom that is being dramatized. The principle of dramatizing prevents its victims from realizing that they are in pain and avoids any show of discomfort. It is therefore more difficult to recognize.

Parents will complain most frequently about insolence on the part of their adolescent offspring. Many times the only thing needed is reassurance that such insolence is a normal attempt on the part of the youngster to break family ties in his awkward efforts to grow up. Defiance of the parents falls into this same category.

One psychiatrist I know found a solution that few parents could ever imagine—or afford! His teen-age son took his car out and "accidentally" backed into a tree. While his father's car was in the shop, he took his mother's car out and "accidentally" backed into the same tree. They bought *him* a car, and he has never put a scratch on it from that day to this. It takes courage (and money) to do a thing like that, but it gives the boy the thing he needs supremely, the certainty that his parents trust him even when he cannot trust himself. You may need some of this same courage with your counselees who, though older, will tend to display some of this same dramatizing behavior when they start to get better. Perhaps more than any other one thing, the minister who does personal counseling needs to learn how he can stand patiently by while the counselee makes his own mistakes and accepts the responsibility for them. This same quality is needed by both the counselor and the parent of the adolescent.

I know one parent, not too old a person herself, whose young daughter stamped her foot and said to her, "I hate you."

She looked back at her, and in a bland way she replied, "You hate me?"

"You're an old goose!" screamed the daughter.

"I'm an old goose?" queried the mother, in the best clinical fashion. Very few parents have the ability to take as casually as this these desperately flung efforts at independence.

Another problem area for parents of this age group and for their counselors is that of poor or declining grades. Any time an intelligent individual begins to make poor grades he should be given a thorough checkup, his physical condition gone over by a competent physician, and his eyesight and hearing tested. Then, if one is available, the school psychologist should be called in for a battery of tests. At the same time the minister may be continuing his help on the emotional level.

Other problems of adolescence include stealing, sex difficulties, and the use of drugs. One of the young patients treated at the hospital where I worked was suffering from what she dramatically designated as "my weakness"—she would steal at every opportunity, but always from her mother, or from a friend of her mother, and always in such a manner as to be caught. Adolescent stealing is often done in such a way that the object is obviously to get caught. One boy in an industrial school escaped, stole a car, drove it all around town, finally went out on the highway, ran it into a tree, and then droppel off to sleep until the tardy police found him and hauled him back to the institution! The thief is usually attempting in the only way he knows to get love and attention. When you are called by the parents, if you take care not to condemn you will soon find in their attitude a cause for the delinquency of the child.

"Is this to mean," you ask, "that young people are to assume no responsibility for their misdeeds?" Indeed not, but if you can realize, and help their parents realize, that here is an act with more than moral implications you may help to guide the punishment into constructive rather than vindictive channels.

Let us go back to our old friend Dr. Jones: when "little Morris," aged thirteen, came home boasting that he'd slid into the afternoon movie without being seen, Dr. Jones said, "Come on, Morris, we're going down there, and I'll wait for you in the car while you go in and pay that young lady and tell her what you did. Our family does not steal or cheat." Some years later Morris Jr. told me himself, "It was the hardest thing I ever had to do in my life, but it cured me of stealing."

Sometimes adults find it hardest to be helpful in matters involving sexual activity. Like it or not, there are times when young girls get pregnant, and the tried-and-true solution of the shotgun wedding may create more problems than it solves, as in the case of Mrs. Drake.

Young people sometimes exhibit a moralistic attitude more firm than that of their parents. Mrs. Barnes wasn't supposed to know that Marvin's girl had pretended to be pregnant in order to get a wedding ring, but in the way of mothers she knew it, so she said casually, "Marvin, if you ever have the bad luck to get a girl pregnant your father and I will support you; we'll pay for the abortion, but we won't let you be forced into an unwanted marriage that will ruin your future."

"Abortion! Mother! You'd take a *life?*"

"O.K. Forget the abortion—we'll stand the expense and help get the girl to one of those homes for unwed mothers.

She can give the child for adoption. All I'm saying is, Marvin, don't ever think you *have* to get married. Marriage is with someone you love for joy always."

"Thanks, Mom." He laughs. "If it ever happens you'll be the first to know." Mrs. Barnes is smart. The time for such a discussion is *before* the fact.

Certainly the unborn child has a better chance with adoption by parents who truly want him than with natural parents for whom his arrival spelled disgrace and the death of all hope for a professional education. On the other hand, many young people become pregnant while not yet legally married, though very much in love, and it would be cruel and immoral to take from them this much-wanted child. Into all these situations the minister is sure to be called at some time during his ministry. Believe it or not, all are fairly common occurrences. The important thing at such a time is to remain uninvolved emotionally, withholding judgment as did Jesus when he said, "Where are those thine accusers? . . . Neither do I condemn thee. Go, and sin no more."

When you counsel young people on the verge of marriage, and their parents, you will find that seldom are all six of these people—bride, groom, and four parents—entirely happy with the arrangement. One of them needs your personal interest and support.

How good, really, is premarital counseling? For the couple who want it and from a minister able to give it—fine; for any and all and from every minister—stilted, false, and even harmful. Too often the so-called premarital counseling purveyed in the average church dodges the all-important matter of sex or seeks to minimize it, but once in awhile you run across a minister like Bill who levels with his young couples.

One woman he had counseled said to me, "Pastor Bill gave my husband a good book on anatomy and sex and told him to read it with me before we came to him for our premarital counseling. He talked to us about our families, money, and mutual interests, but the most important thing we talked about was sex. He didn't seem to mind, no matter what we said. At first we felt shy and giggled a lot, but he treated us like grown-ups (which we are, of course—after all, we're married), and soon we felt free to discuss all our feelings with him and, what was more helpful, with each other. As a result, I saw a doctor, was examined, got the pill prescribed, and went into marriage with no fears and knowing we could plan our family at our own discretion and that we understood each other. It was great—just lots of fun and no hurt feelings or disappointments. In fact, we both said our wedding night made us understand why the ancients used to make the act of coitus the height of their worship. Oh, it was beautiful and holy too—but it wouldn't have been if Pastor Bill ha 'n't been the angel to us that he was."

Good old Pastor Bill! May his tribe increase.

Adolescents can go sour in more ways than by getting pregnant. Today the nightmare of parents is the drug problem, while stealing and defiance of authority remain ever-present. Fortunately, most problems of adolescents are temporary. Young people are often an improvement on their parents, and you will be constantly amazed at their resilience. Nothing is more gratifying than working with teen-agers. No part of your service to your congregation brings such rapid and visible results, nothing requires so much restraint. The least tendency to patronize them or preach at them will shut you out of their lives forever. Insincerity is anathema to youngsters, and they can smell it a mile away; but if you take them seriously and sincerely—give them the respect they deserve—your rewards will be great. Remember the words of Paul to Timothy: "Let no man despise thy youth; but be thou an example of the believers."

Sometimes the believers need to be reminded that young people have a right and a duty to rebel against their elders in order to establish an identity for themselves, lest our church

119

life and our society stagnate. Tennyson reminds us, in his *Morte D'Arthur:*

> The old order changeth, yielding place to new,
> And God fulfills himself in many ways,
> Lest one good custom should corrupt the world.

7
O Wretched Man That I Am!

And now before you sits Enrico—squirming infant, grown to manhood. Inside him somewhere, somehow, in that part of him that is called the soul, his life history is indelibly recorded on his being. Inside, somewhere, all the long-forgotten memories lie dormant, all the scenes of childhood: memories of the early days of infancy, of toilet-training, of sexual discovery, dreams of mother-murder, of brother-murder, all the guilt connected with masturbation, all the love and hate, and the conflicts and the miseries that have brought this man to you with the age-old cry of the neurotic on his lips: "That which I would, I do not, and that which I would not, that I do. O, wretched man that I am!"

Enrico is not even dimly aware of the conflicts that exist within him. He only knows that he doesn't feel very good;

he knows, in fact, that he is miserable, and he knows that traditionally, from the dawn of history, man has asked his priest, "Who shall deliver me?" and from him has received the answer: "God will! Thanks be to him."

Enrico expects and wants this answer, but he will be disappointed and not helped a bit if he gets it delivered to him in a short sentence or in a long lecture. To be effective you must *demonstrate* it through long hours of patient listening.

As you listen, many things will happen. Enrico will weep over injustices done him twenty, thirty, or forty years ago; and feelings that have lain buried for a generation will rise up with all the force of yesterday. He will shiver with guilt over some childish misdemeanor, or curse over some still-remembered slight, or rage over some long-broken toy. This grown-up baby who comes to you for help is a composite of all the things that have ever happened to him. He never thinks of any one of them unless something happens to remind him, and yet he is never free of the conglomerate influences of those early years. Sometimes he is more influenced by past experiences than by the realistic necessities of the present day. What he wants to do he absolutely cannot; and what he simply cannot afford to do he somehow finds that he must. He finds that "the heart has its reasons which reason knows nothing of." (Pascal, *Pensées IV.*)

To such a man there is nothing obsolete about the term "demon-possession," and yet he is even lucky if he knows that he is not doing what he wants to do. Sometimes he believes that he is trying to live as he would choose and that *other people* are at fault, or that other people do not understand him. In any case it behooves his counselor to remember that this man is suffering or he would not be here, so listen with sympathy, and make an effort to understand. The things that come in so handy for a Sunday sermon are useless at a time like this: to tell him what he ought to do— he knows, and he would be out doing it if he could, instead of sitting here talking about it. To call on the Lord in prayer or to swing on a limb of the Scripture is to momentarily avoid the issue. But to meet the issue head on takes understanding, and understanding must be based on knowledge.

A mist of forgetfulness covers the experiences of the early years, and yet through the mist the reaching fingers of the most impressive memories will steer a little track through the rough seas of Enrico's personality. There is a part of every human being that is completely out of his control, yet in whose control indeed he is. In Bible times, as we have mentioned, this was called demon-possession; even in the present day, we find people saying, "God told me to do that," or "A voice told me to do that." In everyday language we just say blankly, "I can't imagine why I ever did such a thing."

Freud called it the unconscious, John L. Lowes called it the Deep Well, but today we can understand it better if we simply say that we have the greatest little computer in the world right between the ears, and all that stored-up material is simply our memory bank. In it are stored the remembered and the unremembered events of our lives, perhaps even as far back as our very conception. Only God knows how much feeling memory is carried in the genes. Certainly they "remember" the color of our ancestors' eyes and hair, the facial and bodily features that make one family different from all other families in the world.

We know certainly that each living person remembers in a feeling way the earliest events of his personal history and in pictures of the mind the events from two and three years of age and up.

Like any other computer our memory bank cannot include anything that has not been once fed into it. Nothing stored within us that has not at one time been conscious. Remember the childhood fantasies? But now as you look at your full-grown counselee his memory of those things is blurred. He has "forgotten," though in another sense he can never forget anything.

The unremembered or rejected feelings and events of our lives seem to live a separate life of their own within us, for our whole self demands to be expressed. When we refuse to acknowledge any but the "nice" part of our personality we start a rebellion within. There are things we "forget" but which refuse to be forgotten. There are memories in a lifetime which can be recalled at will with all the clarity of yesterday; others are like the things we see with the so-called "tail of the eye" or "out of the corner of the eye." Other things are so deeply buried that we are unaware of their existence. In between these last two are the "screen memories," which overlie and represent the earlier memories or the more painful ones. But, unconscious though they be, these early, forgotten experiences still influence and often hamper your counselee's present life—and even your own! Remember that many of the problems that are crucial in the life of a child and that he carries with him into adulthood are met and dealt with before the child can talk or think logically. That is why he bears with him into adulthood so many inaccurate ideas and so many unnecessary anxieties.

Another way of putting it might be to say that all our personal history is like a reel of movie film. We watch only one scene at a time, but as the operator can turn the movie forward or back, so can we recall certain incidents. Unfortunately (or fortunately?) we have never learned to turn our life-movie forward. Sometimes flashes of forgotten things return unbidden to our mind: a scene, a smell, a sound will bring back a whole string of recollections, some related not so much to the original stimulus as to one another. More often we react to the stimulus with feelings we cannot understand or with words we certainly did not expect to say.

Lavinia was a spare-framed, graying school principal, and she told me of such an experience.

"I went to a parsonage tea," said Lavinia. "Everyone was quite dignified, and so was I. I went down the line shaking hands of people I knew slightly and pretending to be pleased to see them. Eventually I came to the superintendent of the city schools who is a great family man. He has himself photographed for the church paper with four generations; he thinks *family* is quite a thing. Personally, I wish sometimes I had one, but it irritated me when he beamed down at me and said in his genial way, 'And Miss Lavinia, did you have a lovely Christmas with your family?'

"He's my boss. He should *know* I'm a loner. I answered brusquely, 'I have no family,' and attempted to move on, but he exclaimed, 'No family!' in what was obviously shocked horror.

" 'No,' I replied evenly, hanging onto my irritation and embarrassment, 'no family.'

" 'No family!' he said as if to a schoolboy he knew to be lying.

"Suddenly I heard myself saying evenly, 'No family, Mr. Stamps; I was *hatched* from an *egg!*' And he's my *boss!*"

The phrases, "I heard myself saying . . ." or "I found myself doing . . ." are familiar idioms in our language. We often do or say something quite at variance with our known plans or desires.

Some acts prompted by unrecognized feelings can have more serious consequences.

The phone on my desk rang. "You know Jessie Jones?"

"Yes, why, hello, Mrs. Marlowe. How is Jessie?"

"Oh, you hadn't heard. She was returned to the hospital yesterday."

"I'm sorry."

"I'm sorry, too, but I had to do it, you know. She lives next door to me."

"Yes."

"Well, she used to come over and talk about music by

125

the hour and play my grand piano. I'm a musician too, and when she asked me to come over and sit beside her and try a duet I thought nothing of it."

I began to suspect what was coming. I knew Jessie's record and that she was supposed to have homosexual tendencies. I also knew Mrs. Marlowe, who like many ladies of her generation was fairly naïve about a good many things. She continued.

"I sat beside her and we began. Suddenly she threw her arms around me and squeezed me so hard I couldn't breathe and began *kissing* me! Oh, Miss Long, I was scared. I didn't know what to do."

"What *did* you do?"

"I got up with her hanging onto me and said I had to go to the bathroom. From there I called and told her I didn't feel well and could I excuse myself and would she come back later. When she left I called the police and had her returned to the hospital. I am ashamed of what I did next. I went next door when the police came and pretended to be surprised at what was happening. I told Jessie I'd come and see her every day."

"Well, I wouldn't blame myself too much. You were in a sort of panic and you did what you thought you had to."

"That's not all. I haven't told you yet why I'm calling you. Last night I got up to get a glass of water and I fell downstairs and broke my leg. So I'm calling to ask if you'll tell Jessie I can't come see her as I promised."

"I certainly will. And I'm sorry you broke your leg."

"Oh, I'm so disgusted with myself! You'd think after living in a house for twenty years I could find my way around it in the dark."

Besides the obvious device of breaking her leg, Mrs. Marlowe could have been doubly distressed because of the response she felt in her own heart to the advances of Jessie. A woman her age, widowed many years, living alone without affection of any kind, could easily have felt her heart leap in response and be afraid that she too might have some homosexual tendencies.

It does seem that she could find her way about in the dark, but see how many problems were solved by the simple expedient of breaking a leg: she neither had to keep her promise to visit the girl whom she did not want to see, nor did she have to break her promise—instead she broke her leg. This will undoubtedly seem like sheer foolishness to some readers, but believe me, friends, many a leg has been broken in a lesser cause! Our motives are usually hidden from ourselves, and in the next chapter we shall look into some of the mechanisms by which we keep them hidden.

In ancient times writing materials were scarce, and ink was perishable. The reeds of the Nile were made into papyrus —thin sheets that rolled out—on which the ancients wrote books laboriously by hand. After some years the ink faded out, and the papyruses were used again for other books. Years later the same thing happened. Three or more books had been written over one another, and when modern man developed the chemical know-how these palimpsests were treated so as to bring back the original writing. You may be doing something like this in your counseling. Conrad Aiken says:

> The pages of our lives are blurred palimpsest: . . .
> The old shines through the new, and colors it.

As you listen you will find that your counselee suddenly is overcome by the memory of an earlier time—or retreats into that other time and begins to talk to you and act toward you as if you were someone else. Unlike the chemist who brings out the exact copy he is seeking, you will find your counselee jumps without warning from one era in his life to another, from one character to another. One time he will talk as if you were his mother, at another he will talk as if

127

you were the historic church. It's up to you to catch on who you are and how old your counselee is each day as first one and then another part of his memory bank reveals itself to you. It may seem a little strange at first, yet the necessity for such a storage tank becomes obvious if you will do the following simple mental exercises:

1. Try to remember everything you did yesterday—*everything*. You see, in general you can remember the day well enough—it may be a day that for some reason you say you will never forget—but to remember every detail of every moment would take as long as it took to live the day in the first place. Yet at different times different things you did yesterday keep popping up into consciousness just because you have set yourself this task.

2. Try to remember everything that happened to you before you were three years old. Some very bright people can remember a few things. Most of us can remember nothing of those years. They are lost in the mist; yet think how important they were in the life of the child that was you. The feeling tone toward the most important things and people in your life was set during that time.

3. Think of your favorite food. What memories do you have regarding it? Doubtless there will be many happy associations not connected with that food in anyone's mind except your own. Mark this well, for association is one of your most useful tools in counseling. It is not always just what your counselee says that helps you to understand him, but in what *connection* he says it—what goes before and what follows after—which will give you the key you need.

4. Think of the most painful physical experience you can recall in childhood. Can you remember just exactly *how the pain felt*? No. You will remember who was there, what they were wearing, what kind of day it was, odors, and many other details, but to remember just how the pain felt would

be to experience the pain all over again with the acuteness of the day it happened.

Forgetting serves many purposes: one is economy, as you saw in exercise No. 1; another is the relief of suffering, as in No. 4. The most painful experiences are those most readily and completely forgotten. Much, in fact most, of what we know is forgotten.

Remember the redwood tree? The marks of past years still show in the layers of forgotten memory. We find that some of our years, like those of the tree, are fat and happy, some are lean and meager—here the death of a loved one, there the bitter loss of another who, though still living, has betrayed our trust: some impression is left by the events of the world's history, but more by the very personal events that have significance only for the individual.

Most of the layers are made up of alternate hostility and love. As a child begins his life he is naturally loving and responsive; if he is repulsed by neurotic adults he covers over this spontaneous *joie de vivre* with a layer of false indifference or with hostile withdrawal. It is the job of the counselor to uncover, bit by bit, and with all the feeling that accompanied its development in the first instance, the earliest layer of spontaneous, loving responsiveness and enthusiasm. I call it peeling an onion, and I can imagine that at the very heart of the onion sits our counselee just waiting to be found. It is quite fascinating to observe these layers peel off one by one as the counselee learns more and more to trust his counselor, for as each layer is discarded the counselee will suffer acutely as if he were tearing out a part of himself, although in reality it is only a part of the neurotic superstructure. He fights to retain the only behavior he has found to be safe. Sometimes he tells the same story over and over again in his effort to master the emotions connected with this particular event.

The live one inside is often a better person than the one we acknowledge. Remember the cages built around the personality? Inside all those cages lives the personality as God meant it to be, and our counselee often helps us to help him discover that person.

The purpose of counseling is to take the veil away from the memory bank and coordinate the forgotten with the present reality so that one is no longer possessed. You may say that one's sins are forgiven or that he has achieved atonement—he is at one with himself—thereby making it possible for him to be at one with God and his fellowman; we may say that he is victorious over this unconscious of his. To say that he is well-adjusted falls rather short of the real accomplishment. To say that he is saved, old-fashioned though it may sound to some readers, is a much more expressive term. One counselee said to me, a bit wonderingly, "You know, it's like being born again." What we are actually doing is helping the counselee, through the use of words and through the use of our own personal relationship to the counselee (see Chapter 8), to remember the things that have troubled him, and to help him work through the anxieties and hostilities of other years which hamper his present life. Working-through is a term that means re-living on a more acceptable level. To review in one's mind the causes of one's illness is helpful, but it does not cure. To live again an experience with all the acute feelings of other years and yet to experience thereby a sense of relief is the real goal of anyone entering into a course of psychotherapy, and to help the counselee to do just that is the goal of anyone giving psychotherapy. The result will be a person who is not tossed about by every whim of his unconscious, but who is actually in full possession of his own soul and accepts responsibility for his own behavior.

"Pastor, what do you think of Jesus walking on the water?" Earnest hazel eyes blinked out of a square, honest face.

"Why Lee, what makes you interested in his walking on the water?"

"Some of the kids at school talked about how it was when they went on trips—like floating, flying. I just wondered if that's what Jesus was doing when he went out walking on the water—if he'd had a tab or two of acid or somebody had a trip that was a bummer and while he was stoned he just *thought* he saw him walking on the water. I was just wondering."

"Wondering about yourself, Lee?"

"Who told you it was me?"

"You told me."

"No, man, somebody else told you. Some narc is trying to get me busted. Who is it?"

"You, Lee, nobody but you. The terms you use are those of a doper. I know you play football—you told me your game has been going down, and you told me because you wanted me to know."

"No, man, no way."

"Yeah, man, you didn't *know* you wanted me to know. Remember the old Western movies with the settlers in the blockhouse and the Indians surrounding it? Well, your real self is the settler in the blockhouse. Your habit, your sicknesss, your sin, whatever you call it—your neurosis maybe—anyway, that's the Indians. I'm the cavalry. I'm trying to save you, but I can't help you unless I know more. So your real self (inside the blockhouse) sends up a lot of smoke signals to me on the hill saying, 'Don't believe those Indians (your outside self)—come and get me.' "

The fear of being criticized by others constitutes one of the great problems of neurotic people, and every person is trying his best to make a good showing. It will take a great deal of patience to help your counselee realize that he has nothing to fear, that he will not be criticized, that the counselor will not be impatient or get angry with him, and that the counselor will not (and this is very important) throw him out. Many at first are quite afraid their counselor is going to find them too difficult or too unlovable to continue the relationship. The perceptive counselor will have his ear primed to hear very often hints of the fear this person has that the counselor may not be willing to see him again. And the first hint that he gives is a plea for reassurance that he cannot become so repulsive that the counselor will not allow him to continue to come in and reveal himself.

I would not have you think that all forgotten things are bad or painful things. Faith, a mental patient, was very sick when she came out with, "Do you hear thunder?"

"Yes, very faint and far away."

"Me, too" (testing the reality of her own perception). Then she said in a musing sort of way, "Rain today, sun tomorrow; the rainbow the promise of God's love."

"Why, Faith. That's beautiful! Where did you get it?"

"Oh" (smiling to herself), "I just made it up in my head."

To look at her in her "normal' state you'd never think of her as a creative person. Yet in her psychotic state she writes prose poetry.

I once knew a contractor who bid on big jobs like county courthouses or city schools. He told me, "When we have a big job to do, I always write down a figure first thing in the morning. Then my partner and I work all day; we go through every detail of the cost and agree on a final figure for the bid. Nine times out of ten it will be the figure I put down in the morning! My brain always works in my sleep like that."

It is to uncover the real person within, with all his creativity and confidence, that we do counseling.

Throughout the development of our counselee, mistakes of parents or educators have left their mark. It is at these points that we must be doubly careful lest we make the same mistakes. It is inevitable that we will make mistakes, being only human, but we can try not to make the *same* mistakes the parents made.

It would be useless to peel off the layers his parents wrapped him in, only to wrap him in other layers of our own choosing. Creative people are not so afraid of their own inner lives that they cannot allow them to be expressed in their conscious existence, unlike the counselee who is usually unaware of his problems like the young man in Chapter 8.

We want our people to be able to make decisions for themselves and to accept the responsibility for those decisions. To become aware of what is considered good and socially acceptable is fine enough, but to be able to use one's own judgment is far finer.

The best possible way for a child to learn relationship to authority is by means of the emotion of gratitude. Many a person behaves well in school or at church because of the fear of one parent or another, or some abstract authority like a policeman, the preacher, or God, who has been used as a weapon to increase his fear. Such a person may go through the motions of socially acceptable behavior, but his heart is not in it. It is only when a man knows he is loved and appreciates this fact that his gratitude helps him to develop a tender conscience, so that his "good" behavior is prompted by the realities of his own life rather than by nameless fears of some dark consequence that may happen as a result of his unacceptable behavior. These persons whose consciences are rooted in gratitude are lovable, loving, enjoyable, giving, and helpful. They are normally altruistic, but not so altruistic as to become ascetic. They are normally friendly with authority but not frightened of it.

8

Who Can Understand His Errors?

Imagine a brilliant scene, rich with color. Jesus, the spiritual king of the world, stately in his linen garment, moves through the marketplace surrounded by his admirers. The crowd parts as a figure clad in rich silks darts toward him. The man is wearing rings on the hands he folds in humility as he bows before the young man only months his senior.

"Good Master," he begins, "what shall I do to inherit eternal life?"

Jesus, impatient with all pretense, cuts through the very form of address. "Don't call *me* good. There is one good, that's God."

The silken shiek straightens his back and addresses himself to Jesus on a more man-to-man level.

Jesus continues, "Love God and your neighbors and follow the commandments."

The young man replies without any hesitation, "All these have I kept from my youth up. What next?"

The bland response of the rich young man makes us smile. He is so like your church member and mine. He has come to Jesus, presumably for information as to how he may attain eternal life, but when Jesus tells him what to do, he answers, "Oh, I do that already."

It is hard for us to grasp the fact at first that our counselee will come to us for help and then in every way possible try to sabotage our efforts to help him. Yet everybody does it. The young man says to Jesus what your own counselee says to you: "Tell me more."

What he means is: "I'm not really here to help myself. I want help but I want you to do all the work."

When Jesus gave his counselee a little homework, like "Go, sell all you have and give to the poor and come back," the young man departed from the scene and from history. In all the Scripture he is never seen or heard from again. Even if, as tradition suggests, it is the same rich man who offered his new tomb for the body of Jesus at a later date, the act is still typical of a person who is resisting the help of his counselor—as if a rich gift could buy peace of mind!

As Jesus watches the young man depart, he is sorrowful, but he does not call him back or offer to reduce the terms of the contract. He cannot, unless he is willing to compromise his own convictions.

Before you get too critical of Jesus' rich young counselee think back to the last time you sliced your finger on a piece of paper. Yes, even a cut from a piece of typing paper can be quite painful. A hurt so small demands your undivided attention for a few minutes, and for an hour, more or less, you might shield it from further hurt. Other hurts are more carefully guarded, like a broken bone or a recent surgery wound. Much more is this true of spiritual hurts, and sometimes we protect them so long the protection itself becomes a hurt.

It is the covering of a hurt that makes a fanatic. Remember how Arnie's wife was so ashamed because she wanted to kill him that she went into a fanatic episode? Her fanaticism was needed to cover the hatred and the shame over the hatred.

Just as I was writing these words the morning paper arrived, and in it was an article about a man who had studied the habits of homosexuals and non-homosexuals who get their sexual relief in public men's toilets. He is an Episcopal minister who spent five years in this study, acting as a lookout to protect the clients of the male prostitutes who did a large business in the "tea rooms" as they are called. He declares, "What surprised me was that most of them were like next-door neighbors, not like swishy Queens. They're good church goers; they keep the neatest houses; the cleanest cars; the best mowed lawns. To fend off feelings of guilt and shame they hold up a breastplate of righteousness, an aura of super-respectability. Politically they are significantly conservative. They are militarily hawks. They are ardent supporters of the police and even the vice squads which may eventually make them prisoners. When they are arrested, good constructive lives are destroyed with long jail sentences and suicides."

He continues that we as a society cannot afford to punish such harmless people. It reminds you of your Official Board. How many are covering up "secret sins" with their clean, well-polished appearance and their sound denunciation of all the evils in the church and in the community? You look around the table and you stop at Jim, known around town as Big Jim. How well you remember Jim!

Last spring you tried out one of these confrontation groups. "Newfangled nonsense," Jim called it. You got your son (a

senior at the nearby college) to help you work out a format.
It had been a success as such things go. Some of the partici-
pants had said they "enjoyed" it. Of course, they didn't
know they weren't exactly supposed to *enjoy* it, but that was
all right.

So you had arranged different kinds of confrontations. Jim
decided to come. "After all," he had said, "the Official Board
ought to be represented *once*." That was the night when
the emphasis was on the problems of modern youth, and the
sub-group Jim joined was being led by a couple of kids who
shared a pad without benefit of legal marriage.

"He would!" you said to yourself when you saw him
coming. "Jim's so straitlaced. Why couldn't he have dropped
in on the film? Oh, well."

So Jim had sat down, and the confrontation had begun.
Maggie spoke first in a low soft voice.

"I know it may seem different to you, but we are living
together. I have an apartment which my dad pays for, and
I have a job at the library. Funny, they won't let married
women work, but they let me. Of course, I know too that Del
would be expected to pay the rent if we married. That minute
[snapping her fingers] my money from Dad would cease.
He believes a husband must pay the bills. That's why marriage isn't feasible, so we live together [shrugging her shoul-
ders]. I furnish the apartment, and Delbert furnishes the
car and the groceries. It works out fine."

"What about children?"

"Oh, I'm on the pill."

"Do you want children?"

"Sooner or later. Right now we want to finish college."

Jim had begun to squirm. So I asked Del to talk about
his side of it. He was dressed in a typical college boy outfit,
which looks strange to the elders of every generation. Jim
squirmed even more.

"Well, when we realized we loved each other, we talked

137

about ways and means; we want to finish school. We expect to get married and raise a family when we can—right now it's not practical."

At that Jim could take it no longer. "Practical! *Practical!* What about moral? Hunh? What about moral?" He was screaming.

Del replied in a quiet voice. "I know it doesn't seem moral to you, but it seems even holy to us."

"You young nuts are all alike! You think you own everything. You think you can have anything—that we owe it to you—you—"

Little Miss Manners had spoken softly, "The young shall inherit the earth."

"What?"

"That's true, isn't it? We'll be dead, and they will be here. I loved a boy once—yes, you may all be surprised to hear that, but I was desperately, agonizingly, in love. It was during the depression. We were poor. Our folks wouldn't help us, like yours [smiling at Maggie]. There was no pill. We had to wait. *I* waited, but the next year he married a girl whose parents *would* help; and here I am. I'm *glad* the youth of this generation have worked out a way."

A hush had fallen on the group, and you had begun to wonder if your confrontation had got off the ground after all.

"How do your parents feel about it?"

Big Jim wasn't cooled off yet. "How *would* they feel about it—you tell me just how would they feel. They'd feel like I—" He broke off suddenly, turning red.

Del said, "Well, they aren't too crazy about the idea, but they accept the facts—my parents more than Maggie's. Last time we were at her house, we had to split when her mother had some of the 'girls' in for coffee. Otherwise it works out. They live in their generation, and we live in ours."

Jim was roaring again. "How do you think they like having

to hide their own daughter because they are ashamed of her?"

Suddenly, to everyone's consternation, Big Jim began to cry.

"I ought to know. I've been hiding mine for six months."

"Oh, Jim." It was Miss Manners. "I didn't know."

"Nobody knew. We tried to work it out as you say, but my wife would be so upset. We talked about having them to visit us (they live at Rockland, forty miles away), but if they did, could we let them share Tina's bedroom? And if we did that, what about the younger children? So I just go down occasionally. Mary won't go at all. I'm beginning to think of them as married, but Mary is very bitter. It's breaking up my own home—" A big hand scruffed up the side of his face, pretending it wasn't rubbing away the tears.

Tears had been in many eyes, including Del's and Maggie's —you had *really* had a confrontation, and you had learned a thing or two yourself. You'd always remember that secret sins are a real problem sometimes. As in the case of Big Jim, the "sins" are kept secret with full awareness of the act. In others the person himself is the last to suspect that he even has any secret faults.

By now you are thinking of your Official Board again. People who cover their secret sins with a mask of self-righteousness often find their way on to your Official Board. They are apt to be quite irritating, but please don't forget that these people are suffering, like George.

"When that guy prays he acts like he's saying, 'Now God, now God, you listen good and do what I want—*or else* . . .'"

"Yeah, ole George is a religious fanatic all right."

"Religious?"

"Well, fanatic anyway."

I knew George—how well I remembered that I, too, had been impatient and a little amused at his fanaticism, until I found myself confronted by him on my doorstep at midnight. The evening was warm, but George was shivering. His teeth actually chattered as he said, "I've got to talk to you." He didn't seem to realize the time.

"Of course, come in."

"Can we walk? I'd rather not come in."

"Of course." I closed the door behind me.

"Here's a bench. Let's sit here."

The night air was heavy with the scent of magnolias, a half-moon rode toward the west, a mockingbird was singing. I was glad somebody had got me out of the house. George saw none of the loveliness. He looked at me with desperate, dull eyes.

"You know the time I talked to you after church about my faith?"

"Yes."

"You said I must be covering up a lot of anger?"

"Yes."

"Well, I have been thinking about it, and the more I think about it, the more I know how right you are. Tonight I was praying, and I began to see myself doing things I couldn't bear to think of doing."

"Saw yourself?"

"In my mind."

"Oh."

"That was why I was praying, and always before prayer has warded off those thoughts, but tonight nothing helped, so I came to you. Will you pray with me?"

Sometimes a request for prayer is just another way of postponing the conversation, but this time I decided to comply.

"Dear Lord, give George the courage to face his thoughts and feelings, for we know you made George and within thy own creation we can find nothing to fear. Help him to remember that you love him exactly as he is and will help to lift the load that burdens him tonight. In Jesus' name. Amen."

George's eyes were no longer dull. They glistened with tears as he squeezed my hand and said, "Thank you."

We sat silent for awhile.

"Tell me, George, what are these things you see yourself doing that frighten you so."

"Oh, I could never—"

"All right. You don't have to say anything if you don't want to." (Using the soft sell.)

We sat another silent while.

"I just get so scared I might not confine those things to thoughts—so scared I might *do* some of those things." (Now he's telling me he really wants to tell me, so I help him.)

"Some of what things?"

"The things I think about."

"What things do you think about?"

"Oh, rape—murder—I imagine I'm Jack the Ripper, and I remember some pretty young girl I've seen within the last few hours. Then I imagine I'm ripping her belly open." He paused and shot a covert look at me.

"Do you always kill young girls in your daydreams?"

(Now I'm telling him, "I'm not afraid of your thoughts, George.")

"No." (Pause.)

"Who, then?"

"Well, tonight it was you. That's why I was afraid to come in the house. I thought if I got out of control in the open you could run or scream, and help would come."

(Thanks a lot, George!)

"Do you have sexual desires toward me, is that it?"

"Yes."

"And do you think sex is dangerous?"

"Yes. My mother and father never had sex until they had had a terrible fight first. I used to lie in my room and listen to them and the horrible names they called each other, and hear him knocking her around and her crying, and then

141

things would get very still for awhile and soon the bed would begin to squeak, and I'd know it was over for the time being; but I was always so scared that someday he'd hit her too hard or knock her against something sharp, and sometimes I wished they'd kill each other. I *hated* those people—living in that house was hell!"

The memories of George's childhood were too painful—but his defense against them was more painful. We learn to defend ourselves against pain in other ways. For instance, we "forget it" sometimes past recall, yet it continues to cause trouble; or we deny its very existence ("I'm not crying," yet the tears are rolling down); by dramatizing it ("Out damned spot. Will this little hand never be clean?"); by remembering a happier time; by the sour grapes technique; by postponing it ("I'll worry about that tomorrow"); and by acts of rebellion against society.

Most of these modes of behavior are not recognized by the person who performs them as a means of protection against hurt. If we can show them what they are doing and why, they may be better able to help themselves—but a mere "interpretation" of their "problem" is not enough. I like Jesus' method of giving homework, and I practice it quite often.

Jesus dealt with his counselees realistically. Remember another scene in which we find him at the Sheep Gate of Jerusalem at the time of a Jewish religious feast. At the Sheep Gate is a pool (probably some kind of a hot spring that became disturbed at irregular intervals), and around the healing pool the people have built a wall with five porches. Someone has informed Jesus that a man who has been ill for thirty-eight years lies hopefully beside the pool. They have asked Jesus to help him. Jesus now walks in among filthy, ill, and ill-smelling hunks of humanity; picking his way carefully, he arrives at the spot where his friend's friend lies waiting. Jesus looks at the man, and the man looks back at him. Jesus speaks first.

142

"Do you want to get well?" It sounds like a cold question, but listen to the answer:

"Sir, I don't have anyone here to put me into the pool when the water is stirred up; while I am trying to get in, somebody else gets there first."

Notice that he does not acknowledge that he wants to get well; neither does he say he does not want to get well. Instead he tries to tell Jesus what a hard time he has; he is apologetic for not having availed himself of the opportunities he has had to get help. His guilt implies that he probably is enjoying poor health. Jesus ignores the pool and the excuses of the patient. Instead he says in effect, "Today is a new day—we are not going to worry about what you haven't done before—we are going to get on with getting you taken care of today, but first, you must show me that you are willing to make an effort." So he gives his man a little homework: "Take up your mat and walk."

The story has a surprise ending and a happy one. The man did take up his mat, and he did walk! The great charm and power of Jesus had worked again. But don't expect such instant success of yourself. Most parishioners ask for help, tell you a few things, and immediately begin to be sorry they ever talked to you. This they show by telling you they are fine now, or by becoming angry with you, or by telling you they have found a better counselor, or by saying they cannot spare the time. Many more excuses could be listed but all are saying the same thing:

"I'm scared. I have told you things I never told anybody. Things I didn't know myself, things about myself I don't even want to know, and I'm running as fast as I can to get away from these frightening inner feelings."

But don't become discouraged. Whatever you do, don't become irritated. Your counselee would do better if he could. He does want to get well. He just doesn't know how. He is counting on you for that. *You* know he is trying to sabotage your efforts to help him, but he doesn't. He will become bewildered and hurt if you assume his resistance to be a diabolically perverse attitude on his part. He only knows he wants help. That he is afraid of getting help, that he is frightened, that he is hiding hurt or protecting himself from further hurt—all these facts are unknown to him.

Jesus was confronted by this problem also. As he sat by Jacob's well, a woman approached. In a town the size of Sychar it is unlikely that she did not know who this man was. With his usual acumen Jesus knew she had pretended to come to draw water, but actually had come to see him. So like a good counselor he said to the woman, "Give me a drink." (Known in some circles as "establishing rapport.")

Immediately her defenses are up.

"You are a Jew, and I am a Samaritan. Good Jews don't speak to Samaritans. What's the matter with you?" (Or to be exact, "When I came to see you, I hoped you'd talk to me, but now that you're doing it, I'm scared. Let's see if I can divert you into a discussion of racial and sectional prejudice.")

He refuses to be diverted from the main subject. "If you knew who is asking, you would ask *me* for a drink of water; for if I should give it to you, you would have a well of water springing up inside of you that no man could stop, and you would never again have inside of you that awful thirst that makes you do such strange things."

Pretending not to catch on, she tried to talk about the well and Jacob who built it, and to question the ability and authority of Jesus. (Sometimes your counselee will ask you to explain just how you happened to get into the ministry, where you got your training, etc. He is trying to belittle you—to put you on the spot.) Jesus didn't take the bait.

By now some of her problems are obvious.

"Go fetch your husband." Many counselors even today like to talk to the whole couple.

For once she gives him a straight answer, "I have no husband."

"You can say that again! For you have had five husbands, and the man you are living with now is not your husband."

For a moment Jesus seems to have scared off his client.

"Sir, I perceive that you are a prophet, and so you can settle an argument that has been plaguing this valley for a long time. Our fathers worship on this mountain, but you say that Jerusalem is the only place that God can be worshiped." (If all else fails, get him into a theological argument—*that* will take the heat off.) But Jesus refuses to fall into the trap.

"Neither on this mountain nor in Jerusalem, for the place is not important. God is a spirit, and his worshipers must worship him in spirit if they are to worship him in truth."

Timidly, tentatively, then she tries out her new-found trust.

"You must be the Messiah." Her defenses are fully down now.

These defenses thrown up by your counselee remind me of the old Maginot Line in France. After World War I the French were determined to protect themselves against all future attack (they, like your counselee, did not expect circumstances to change so drastically in a few short years). By the time World War II came along things were different— very different. Land warfare was on its way out. The planes of the Germans had brought the French to their knees long before the Maginot Line was even more than dented. It was worse than useless, for it diverted money and troops that should have been used to protect the border in a more effective way. The Maginot Line proved to be no more than an expensive, cumbersome white elephant.

Remember that, like the Maginot Line, your counselee's defenses were originally built up against a real and present danger, but as time went on and circumstances changed, the defense became obsolete—it became too much for the personality to protect that and the more real hurts of the present time, and it became for him a white elephant that the counselee did not even know he had.

Sometimes we condense meanings into symbols, such as the cross, the flag, the praying hands. Our whole society recognizes and reacts emotionally to these familiar symbols, but they can be used to defend one against pain too.

Max was one of a group of students in a lecture. He was quite upset—all had made comments about the lecturer, who talked with a gimlet eye fixed on first one student and then another, but Max made the unique comment, "It makes me feel like a gun that is being cleaned out." To arrive at his meaning without frightening him, I asked, "Can you think of another time when you felt that way?" "Yes," came the reply. "I had a Scoutmaster once—" There followed a story of how this Scoutmaster used to quiz the boys about their habits of masturbation, eliciting from them all the details; later it developed that this same Scoutmaster, himself, had homosexual tendencies. My counselee was about to engage in more normal sexual activity, as he was in the process of falling in love with one of the girls in the community, but to him it seemed that this might be unacceptable to the authority (in this case represented by the lecturer). All his fear of detection and all his guilt over his earlier childhood behavior were expressed in the symbolic statement, "I feel like a gun that is being cleaned out."

In these and other ways the counselee fools himself and attempts to fool you. Remember, he *believes* he is trying to be open and honest with you, and he longs for your help. His relatives may tell you, "He knows better." But if he knew better, he would do better. He sits there wasting your time telling you he can't think of a thing to say, but you know that what he is trying to say is so painful that he dare not even know himself what is on his mind.

So you wait patiently, and you sit looking at each other.

Your counselee is begging for help while he fights it every step of the way. He clings to his misery because that is the only way of life he knows. To him it seems that to cut out his pain is to cut out a part of himself, and so he fights you and he begs you not to let him go.

Can you look on this young man and love him? Can you demand that he give up his dearest possession—his neurosis—in such a way that he will not "go away sorrowful" but will take up his bed and walk? Can you help him understand his errors and be cleansed of his secret sins? If you can, you will understand the Master when he told his disciples, "No, I haven't eaten, but I'm not hungry. I have had meat to eat that you know nothing about."

9
Cleanse Thou Me from Secret Faults

We have discussed the normal development of any individual and some ways in which the normal may be buried beneath the habits needed to defend oneself against faulty upbringing or the unplanned events of life that come to every growing thing. Now let us look at ways in which the results of spiritual hurts may be erased or compensated so that the counselee is brought back to a natural expression of his emotions.

To reach the real personality beneath layers of sweet obsequiousness, flaming anger, and entrenched bitterness, the counselor must endure the expression of all the pent-up hostility of the years.

Not long ago I watched a play in which a very ugly man was engaged to a blind girl. An operation was performed on her eyes, and she sat eagerly looking toward the man so that her first sight would be of the one she loved, but before the last bandage was taken off he turned and ran from the room in a panic. He just could not believe that this woman could love him if she ever saw him as he was! This is a thumbnail sketch of every person who comes to a counselor. It is the common denominator of all emotionally disturbed individuals. The one thing they need above all others is to have someone demonstrate to them that even though he sees them exactly as they are he can love them just the same. The moment you begin to moralize or criticize or show irritation, you are by your action saying to this person, "You are right. Your personality is so ugly that no one can tolerate it as it is." As counselors our first task is to tolerate the silly fears, the infantile rages, the masturbation, and the illicit loves—*all* behavior of our counselees. Faith in God and faith in humanity must be our resource at this point. The words of Jesus come down to us—"Neither do I condemn thee"—and give us strength to hold back the reproaches that rise so readily to our lips.

Ida said in amazement, "You mean I can use aggression like gas in the gas tank? Let it explode a bubble at a time and it carries me wherever I want to go?"

"That's right."

"And if I try to hold it in, it gets too big for me and I have an explosion—or try to be sneaky with it and it backfires?"

"You're catching on."

"Just express my anger when I feel it? About the real thing that made me angry and it goes away—hold it in, it grows?"

"Yes."

Ida laughed. After a few more sessions she came up with, "My husband said something I didn't like. He has said it a thousand times before and I never liked it, but this morning I found myself suddenly throwing my cup of coffee, saucer and all, at him." She laughed. "I will never forget the expression on his face when he saw that cup and saucer sailing through the air. He looked so funny. Then I broke down and told him a few of the things I'd never dared to tell him before about his irksome ways. You know, I think he liked me better for it."

The note of wonderment frequently creeps into the voices of those who practice these "theoretical" methods and find them to actually work out in everyday life. The more bitterness and rebellion are driven underground, the greater the need for counselors who fear neither the aggression of their counselees nor their own. Acceptance at this point will bring greater rewards than at any other level of the counseling process. A hostile expression, particularly against the counselor or members of his immediate family, may represent growth. Reassurance at such a time could be honestly expressed in a sympathetic way, such as, "Perhaps everyone feels like that at some time or other."

Often a counselee tells of experiences or behavior that might not be too desirable. At such times a quiet response, a question, or just waiting may lead into a deeper level of feeling than would taking a stand at once on what seems to be a moral issue.

Henry sat down. He looked tired and angry.

"My wife wanted me to talk to you," he says defiantly. "She's furious at me because I can't buy her a new dishwasher. Why should she have a dishwasher? My mother never had one. I don't do anything now with my money but spend it on that woman and her house. This morning I got sick of her eternal nagging, and I belted her one right in the mouth. That's when she said if I didn't come talk to you, she'd leave me."

"Yet you are here."

"I had to come. She said she'd leave home unless I did come."

"I don't believe you, Henry."

"What!"

"You want to say she forced you to see me, but if you didn't want to come you wouldn't be here."

"Well—"

"So now tell me your side of it."

When your counselee talks about socially unacceptable behavior it helps to remember that too much has been demanded of him too fast. Antisocial behavior develops as a protective shield against unbearable frustrations, either real and present or fancied and historic. It is as if he had been given a map for buried treasure, and he begins to dig just a small angle off the course. From then on, the harder he digs, the farther he goes from the treasure! Most of the persons who come to you for help are beginning to be aware that they are digging in the wrong direction. To tell them that this is so will not help them much; to get in the ditch with them and "help" them to continue to dig with more vigor in the wrong direction is to harm rather than to help them. When someone comes to us whose symptoms are socially unacceptable—like kleptomania, alcoholism, homosexuality, or promiscuity—he or she is usually condemning himself already; to reprove him or try to "convert" him, thus making him feel that God is reproving him, is like getting in and helping him dig away from the treasure.

In order to demonstrate the love of God it is necessary to hold one's peace and let the counselee talk. To interpret for him that he is eating or drinking or stealing in order to get the love he never had as a child would be like giving him a map for buried treasure written in a foreign language! There is only one way to demonstrate the love of God, and that is to act it out by loving him as you believe God would love him, with a depth of understanding and a degree of acceptance that this person has never known—never rude, pointing out his faults; never selfish, insisting that he accept *your* viewpoint; never irritated because he cannot understand;

giving yourself no airs, pointing out how much you know about his unconscious feelings; never gladdened when others go wrong; never saying, "I told you so"; always eager to believe the best, by trying to understand *why*. Thus love, interpreted by your behavior, will never fail.

When a counselee describes his hostile feelings toward someone else in great detail, he frequently is hinting that his real hostility is toward the counselor; when he tells you bad things others have said about you, though he defended you to the end, he is really saying, "I hate you, so I'll tell you all the bad things I can collect that people have said about you—but *other* people. I'm scared to tell you, myself."

Or when the counselee responds to the question, "How did it make you feel?" by saying very quickly, "Well, I'm not sore," or "I'm not angry with my mother," or some other sudden unexpected denial not brought on by any statement of the counselor, then the counselee is obviously finding this material within himself. Such slips of speech are a valuable tool in the hands of a skilled counselor, and can be used to great advantage for the healing of this ailment of hostility, which provides so much difficulty in the lives of both counselee and counselor.

What are the ways in which a counselee indicates that he has angry and hostile feelings and in what ways can the counselor encourage the expression of these feelings? One of the easiest places to look is in the direct relationship between the counselor and the counselee. In fact, every statement that is made by the counselee can conceivably be interpreted on three levels: the present, the past, and the immediate relationship in which he finds himself. The one least likely to provoke unmanageable anxiety on the part of the counselee is his relationship to you. Much of the work that is to be done with this person must be done right in your office as he expresses again and again his feelings toward you, but it will not be done without encouragement and assistance from you. What, then, are his attitudes toward you which may show a hostile reaction?

The first and most noticeable of all is a reaction of silence; the managing of silence, as has been pointed out previously, is one that requires artistic skill on the part of the counselor. A remark to the effect that this silence on the part of the counselee is probably produced because he feels hostile toward the counselor sometimes brings amazing results. The counselee may deny that he has any hostile feelings; he should be allowed to sit and feel the weight of the silence for himself after the first suggestion on your part that it probably stems from hostility. The weight of silence is a real strain for some ministers, but it is an even greater strain for the counselee and if allowed to go on long enough will result in some statement by him which may be quite revealing. If this silence, on the other hand, is continually broken by the counselor, the counselee has very little opportunity of revealing what is going on in his mind.

One of my students found that his patient sat without speaking for almost the entire therapeutic session. He came back to report to the group that he thought he would change patients since this one seemed not to have much to say, but on being quizzed a little, the following facts were revealed: this visit was the first that the patient had received from this particular student in three weeks. The student on approaching the patient had said casually, "I'm sorry, but I have been very busy and have not been able to see you." The student then commented that the only thing that the patient had said during the whole hour was, "A minister from the Church of God in a nearby town came to see me." Immediately his fellow students pointed out the fact that this patient had said quite a bit in that one brief statement. In other words, he had given the student his reason for silence. "*You* have not been to see me, but another minister has been to see me." If the student had at that time said quietly, "And you feel angry because of this neglect on my part," no doubt the silence would have given way to quite a bit of conversation!

Another way in which hostility is expressed, oddly enough, is through the bringing of gifts to the counselor. When a counselee begins to bring gifts in or send gifts in excess of reasonableness (in other words, more often than once a year!) he is expressing guilt over feelings of hostility. Although one of the most difficult things that the counselor has to do, it is incumbent upon him at this point to suggest to the counselee, "You must feel hostile toward me, or you would not need to bring me presents." Undoubtedly this will very rapidly bring the hostility to the surface, and it will certainly result in a cessation of the flow of gifts, but it will encourage a more honest expression of feeling.

A third way in which a counselee shows his hostile feeling is to stop coming altogether, skip a session, call when it is too late for the minister to plan other uses for his time, or come in several minutes late. Even though the counselee says that he is ill, it is still not unfeeling to mention that he may be ill because he wants to avoid looking further into his own soul. A certain amount of toughness is necessary in a situation such as this. A show of firmness on the part of the counselor will not be so painful to the counselee as one might think. The person who is feeling hostile will welcome any degree of hostility on the part of his counselor because this gives him a license to release his own hostile feelings without developing too much guilt. Of course, this is exactly what the counselor is after. We do not deliberately needle a counselee in order to make him show hostility, for this might tend to drive the feelings underground. We simply open a door through which the true feelings of the counselee may emerge. If he does not come at all and does not call, we may give him a couple of weeks and then call him, and ask what's going on.

An expression of undue concern on the part of the counselee for the counselor is usually an expression of hostility, although sometimes it may merely be a desire to get closer to the counselor. The counselee may insist that you look white and pale, or ask if you are sick, or express a fear for you to go to a distant city for a meeting because of the fact that you may have a wreck in your automobile. Any such expressions on the part of an individual of excessive concern for the health and welfare of another indicates an unconscious hostility. Remember Julia, who thought she feared Arnie might get killed, but in reality found she actually wished him dead? One of the more difficult concepts for the average person to accept is this very strange one, in which a fear is shown to be an inverted wish. The wish that someone might die or be sick, or be hurt, or be away and out of one's life, is expressed at times through a fear that this may happen. Thus, in effect, the person expresses his guilt in advance for the deed that his mind would like to commit. We are now dealing with one of the feelings that we described earlier: that of omnipotence, which expresses itself through a fear that the wish alone may produce the deed, so that a feeling of intense guilt arises over an even unconsciously hostile thought. Do not be afraid to wade in with all four feet at this point and indicate to the counselee his hostile feeling, especially toward you as his counselor. Sometimes to tell a counselee that he would like to have his wife dead or out of the way, or that he wishes his children unborn, is too strong a dose of medicine for him to take, but you are always safe in pointing out that he feels hostile toward you, thus giving him an opportunity to work off on a relatively unimportant person in his life the feelings he has toward those closer home.

The average minister's worst blind spot is in this very area of hostility. The fantasy among church people that to express honest aggression is bad keeps us from seeing the value of draining off the bitterness and the hostility in the counselees we meet. When a person's own emotions become involved, they interfere with what he is able to do for his counselee. I remember a very fine counselor who, except in this one respect, was of great help to his counselees, but during an interview in which he was having tea with his counselee, the counselee suddenly became angry and said, "I think I'll just knock you down," at which point the counselor responded, "If you do, I won't see you again." The counselor was well trained and knew that an encouragement of hostility was theoretically very good, but he could not stand the anxiety of the threat that he might get knocked down.

The Christian virtue of moral courage comes in at this point to assist the counselor, even while the misplaced or abnormal fear of hostility deters him from his purpose.

I well remember the first real demonstration I ever had of the fact that moral courage is an active ingredient of human relationships and that it does work, even with greatly disturbed persons. As a student in a mental hospital, I was quite interested in a quiet, soft-spoken little catatonic. On one occasion she was talking to me when a husky patient, an ex-nurse, came up and demanded that I unlock the door and let her out. I looked around for a technician, but there was none in sight. To call for help would frighten the patient who was talking to me, so I looked quietly back at the nurse and said, "I can't let you out." "You can too," she replied. "You have the keys right there in your hand." Indeed, I had the keys in my hand! I just looked back at her quietly with my heart pounding ninety miles an hour, and I said, "I'm sorry." She leaped at me and grabbed for my throat. I stood my ground but didn't move a muscle to counterattack. Her hands clutched at a soft bow on my blouse and pulled it apart. Surprised at her own aggression, she stepped back a pace and said to me, "Are you going to let me out?" And in the same quiet voice I replied, "No, dear." The patient seemed utterly nonplussed by such treatment. My little patient droned on about her own troubles, never noticing that anyone else was present. Needless to say, I edged gradually toward another door and let myself out as quickly as possible.

I dreaded returning to the same ward the next day for fear that my erstwhile attacker would leap on me and batter me to bits. On the contrary, she beamed at me with a great smile and was my friend from then until the end of my student career. This taught me a lesson I will never forget—that after all, soft words do turn away wrath; that moral courage actually works. It works nowhere so well as in the counseling situation.

Not only do we counselors need to accept and tolerate hostility for the good of the counselee, we sometimes actually need to encourage it.

The handling of hostilities comes very much to the fore in the work that ministers do with bereaved families. Death is a traumatic experience for all concerned, and here I pause to return your attention to some statements made earlier about the omnipotent feelings that lie buried in the unconscious and the death wishes that every child has at some time or other felt toward the members of his intimate family circle. Without an understanding that the murder of mother, father, brother, and sister has been contemplated at some time in every individual's past life, one cannot fully appreciate the varied emotions that go into the mourning process. All grief carries with it certain elements that are not entirely unselfish. The person lost is in some way necessary to the emotional pleasure of the person grieving, and thus the grief takes on a certain self-centeredness. One is never entirely altruistic in grief. There is nevertheless a large element of guilt in most grief. Just as it is true that when a new child enters the family, there is both rejoicing and resentment, so it is that when any one member of the group leaves the family, there is both grief and relief. That we can be both sorry and glad that a loved one is gone is totally unacceptable to most of us. We find people able to verbalize this relief only if the illness has been particularly prolonged and the suffering of the departed one has been particularly severe, or if the person who has died was extremely old or mentally or physically handicapped. The relatives of the young to middle-aged, moderately vigorous person, however, find it practically impossible to admit that his going away may be a relief as well as a sorrow. Sometimes when being helped by counseling, a person will voice some of these sentiments.

"I can't do anything with Mother. She's so old, but she can't realize she's not young anymore. Sometimes I think we'd both be better off if I just shot her and got it over with."

I chuckled, "That's cute."

Jill screamed at me, "You don't understand! I'm talking about murdering my mother; there's nothing cute about it."

"Well, you see, if you talk about it you may not have to do it."

"Oh."

Yes, it is true that throughout life anxiety is lessened if we can talk about it to an understanding listener. It is essential, of course, that we as counselors not panic.

I remember one young fellow whose mother was hung like a millstone around his neck by the death of his father and her own poverty. He was not able to move about as he pleased or to marry because his own financial condition would not allow it, and he could not throw the old lady out into the street. Since she was not eligible for an old-age pension, he was actually stuck with her. After a few weeks of counseling he said to me, "You know, death not only creates problems, it solves problems." Such a confession on the part of a counselee must be received with great delicacy by the counselor, lest this stirring awareness of his hostile feelings be frightened back into its lair by the response of displeasure or shock on the part of the counselor. As I remember, I just said, without changing my tone or expression, "Yes, it does."

When the death has actually taken place, the situation is even more delicate. A grieving person must be encouraged to express all his resentment at the loss of his loved one, all his hostile feelings toward life itself, even toward God, for what has happened to him. Gradually, as his grief becomes ameliorated, he may confide that sometimes this person who is gone was a bit annoying at this or that point. It is here that the real healing work begins. The counselee remembers certain characteristics of his lost loved one which he might find it quite convenient to be without. The reverence for the dead that we have always had harks back to a sort of ancestor worship and is certainly anything but reminiscent of the attitude of Jesus: "Let the dead bury their dead and come and follow me." If we ourselves can be less sentimental and more practical about the whole area of grief and mourning, we shall be of infinitely more help to our parishioners.

I'm sure that I don't need to mention that one of the worst things a minister can possibly do at a time like this is to suggest a memorial window or a memorial baptismal font or mention any other way in which he may capitalize financially upon the grief of his parishioner.

Repeatedly in a time of grief over the death of a loved one or the illness or injury to oneself, we hear our people saying, "Why did this have to happen to *me?*" or "What have I done to deserve this?" Both these questions are implied expressions of guilt, and the very delicate task of the counselor at this point is to run down the reasons why his counselee should think this might have happened to him or what he actually *suspects* he has done to deserve this. We tend to be so sentimental at a time of grief or suffering that we give people premature reassurance and comfort without allowing them to ventilate fully their innermost feelings of guilt which they are more likely to do now than at any other time, and thus we cheat our counselees out of one opportunity to confess their real or fancied sins. I say "real or fancied" because so many people are borne down with guilt over small things or feel guilt irrationally at some point that is highly insignificant without having any realistic appraisal of the guilt that they *should* feel for *actual* wrongs done to other people. Such unrealistic guilt needs very much to be relieved.

On the other hand, there are times when guilt not only needs to be expressed and forgiven, but needs also to be felt and responsibility for it accepted. There is such a thing as false and irrational guilt, but there is also such a thing as a quite realistic sense of guilt over a very real injustice done to someone else. I was called once by a minister in a community and asked if I would see a depressed member of his church. She was not hospitalized, but she was in an extreme state of depression. She had cried through two interviews with him when he called me for help. I agreed to see Adelaide, and she came out to the office crying as usual.

"Dr. Hart told you I lost my baby?"

I nodded, "Yes."

"I think I killed her."

"Oh? How's that?" (Suppressing a natural desire to assure her that I'm sure she didn't kill her baby.)

"Well, it was Friday night, and Pearl wouldn't eat her supper. I had to go to a shower, so I went on. Next morning she played a little, so I didn't worry. I had to go to a dance that night, and I spent all day making my dress."

"You *had* to go?"

"Yes, my husband is very bad about that kind of thing. When he says we go out, we go."

"Did you tell him Pearl was sick?"

"I didn't realize how sick she was. I thought she had a cold. I gave her some orange juice—made her drink it and went on to the dance. It was late when we got home. She was crying—kind of whimpering. I gave her an aspirin. She slept late—next morning she slept and slept. We had a family reunion, and so I got her up and dressed her and took her with us. My husband's mom said at the picnic, 'You've got a sick baby, Addie, better let the doctor have a look at her.' But when I called him, they said it would be Monday at nine. By then she couldn't swallow at all. I got in about an hour after we arrived. Soon as we got in the doctor said, 'This child has to go to the hospital.' I asked, 'When?' and he said, 'Right now.' He called an ambulance and they let me ride out with her—but she died before the next morning."

I listened to the same story next day. She told it over and over every time she came to see me, repeating every minute detail of the child's illness and hospitalization. I could not help being impressed with the fact that this woman *had* been rather neglectful and careless in her handling of the child and perhaps *could* have prevented the death if she had been a little more alert to the child's needs, rather than her own. She was an immature girl, rather a young mother and somewhat wrapped up in her own needs without too much concern or motherliness toward her children. Her sense of guilt was definitely justified. However, I did not add to her self-inflicted punishment by agreeing that she had been neglectful. I would ask such questions as, "You feel that you did not suspect how ill she was?" Thus, at the same time that I acknowledged her part in the child's death, I gave her something of an out.

This, however, was not all the story. She told me that her family was very impatient with her and thought that she "cried too much." I asked her how long since this death had occurred, thinking that with so much impatience on the part of the family and such apparently excessive grief on the part of the counselee, it would have been at least several years. She replied to my amazement, "Last month." I told her that I certainly did not think that she cried too much, that I thought the most natural thing in the world was for a mother to grieve over the loss of a child more than one month. It became evident that although she felt a great deal of justifiable guilt over her child's death, this guilt was compounded by her guilt over unbearable hostilities toward her husband, his sister, and his mother. She was able to express a few of her hostile feelings toward these persons remaining in the family circle when I told her that I thought they expected a bit too much of her, and because I was able to criticize the family, she pitched in and criticized them even more. Thus her need was met for an outside person to give her support while she expressed some of this hostility toward the members of the family who were very close to her. When grief seems to be excessive, there is usually more than the death of the person immediately involved to be considered.

There are forms of grief more painful than the sweet clean grief of death.

"I wish they'd brought Mace home from Vietnam in a box!" Sue said in the church prayer group.

"Oh, Sue!"

"Don't be horrified," said the minister. "Let's hear her out."

"Well, if he'd been killed three years ago, if he'd arrived all flag-draped and accompanied by taps—at least I'd have had the sympathy of my friends and his family; and I'd have had precious memories that I could treasure always."

"And now?"

"Now" (bitterly), "there he sits in a beautiful home with a new wife. His relatives still like me, but for anniversaries and special days, they have to have *her* for dinner. Our friends chose up sides when we separated. Some tried for a while to keep up with both of us, but that didn't last. I have custody of the children, but legal custody doesn't mean they *enjoy* a cheap little apartment on poverty row better than the weekends and vacations they spend there with ponies and a swimming pool—and don't think he and Number Two don't play *that* tune to the full limit. Don't misunderstand me; I don't wish him *dead!*"

"Of course you do; you just said so."

"Well, if you put it that way. I don't wish him dead *now* —I wish he'd *been* dead before our marriage ever went sour."

Sometimes depression spells an inner loss—the loss of love within one's self. This is the type of feeling which drives one to the church office wailing, "I am a miserable sinner," hoping the minister will hear the real cry, "I am a miserable *person.*"

Like Julia, these people are not even aware they are angry (except perhaps at themselves), yet they express their anger by acting so openly miserable they make their entire family miserable. They beat their breasts and cry out that they are unworthy of such a wonderful spouse, while all the time they are making the days and nights of the wonderful spouse a living hell. These people must be helped to realize two things: that they are angry, and at whom. Once they are able to make a more honest expression of anger toward the hated person, they begin to lose their feeling of depression fast. Depression is one of the sneaky ways one expresses anger.

Some people use alcohol and drugs in order to whip up the courage to express the same feelings. Often the moral values of such persons are quite mixed up, as in the case of the youngster dedicated to the making of a better world, who saw no conflict in the fact that though he would not touch coffee, coke, or cigarettes he routinely smoked marijuana and took LSD to "expand his mind."

The counselor who works at helping the counselee to a better understanding of his own feelings will eventually bring about a change in his morals and earn his undying love and respect.

10

They Left Their Nets
and Followed Him

The charisma that Jesus had in such abundance is shared to some extent by all of us who counsel others. Of course, it's unlikely that many will abandon their jobs just to follow us, but our counselee will invest us with a Godlike omnipotence. When your counselee comes into your office and sits before you, he already has you identified with all authority: you are his mother, his father, the church, God, his commanding officer in the service, his doctor, the cop on the beat, his teacher—just all *authority!* He will think of you in terms of one of these authority figures every moment of every visit, but is is usually up to you to guess which one you represent at any given time.

Sometimes this situation reminds me of a tourist attraction we have all seen: there is a series of life-sized pictures with no heads, sitting or standing around—one is riding a burro; one is a girl's figure lying on top of the piano; another is down on his knees shooting craps. You stick your head in the blank space, and a photographer snaps you in those strange postures for the amusement of the folks back home. So it often is with you when you do counseling. The counselee comes in and sticks you into the clothing and posture of his father, mother, teacher, or another—and there you sit. To him you represent that person until his feelings change, and then you become someone else. But it doesn't really matter who you seem to be. What you really are does matter a great deal. If you can remain firm in your own identity, your counselee will not be able to force you into a false role, and in that way you will help him to meet a new person; having met one new person (you) he can then drop his rigid feeling that everyone is someone he has known in the past.

Alta looked puzzled.

"You know, I have feelings about you which at the same time do not seem to be about you at all. It is as if I thought about you in two ways—you and someone else."

"That often happens. Such feelings are not uncommon."

"It seems that I have been making fathers and mothers out of everybody all my life."

"Most of us do that without being in the least aware of what we are doing."

"But I expect them—you—to act like my mother or my father and when you don't, I get distressed."

"Yes, the other day when I acted in a different way from what you expected, you got quite angry."

I was referring to the last Wednesday when Alta had called me at 6:00 A.M., saying that she just had to talk to me. I had said, "I'll get dressed and have breakfast and meet you downstairs in an hour."

So at six-thirty she had rung the doorbell. I had dressed, but had not eaten anything. However, I went down. It developed that her problem was not urgent. Her family doctor had told her two weeks before that she would have to have an operation of a minor nature sometime during the next year. But in the night she had dreamed that she died on the operating table, and it had scared her. Though the problem did not seem urgent to me, it seemed so to her. We talked for two hours. We went over the symptoms and her feelings about them; we discussed her family situation with which I was quite familiar; the competency of her doctor; the possibility of a baby sitter for her children; we even discussed pall bearers!

"I don't know whether I ought to go through with it or not," she was saying to herself, when I glanced at my watch and saw that it was eight-thirty already. I said. "Alta, it is getting late. The dining room will be closed in a few minutes. So if you will just sit here and think about it, we can discuss it further when I get back."

She flew into a rage. "Breakfast? *Breakfast?* That's all you think about. Your god is your belly. You're just like all the rest. You don't give a damn about me."

"I guess I would have eaten before I came down in the first place if I really hadn't cared, if my god were my belly. I guess I could just have made you wait at six this morning. Couldn't I?" I was on my feet as I spoke, and I moved toward the elevator as she sat open-mouthed and speechless—I couldn't tell if it was with surprise or rage. But when I got back, she was sitting, thoughtful and repentant. We talked about the fact that she might have been trying without knowing it to keep me there until I did something to let her become angry. She was trying to make a parent out of me.

"I hope I'm not doing that to my husband." (Thoughtfully.)

"Not doing what to your husband?"

"With his drinking."

"I didn't know Joe drank."

166

"He doesn't. That's just it. Once in a great while he goes out for a night with the boys, and he always has a few beers with them those nights. He calls it 'a few beers'—*I* think he comes home drunk. Then I get panicky and am sure that he is going to turn out to be an alcoholic like my father was. He used to come home drunk and beat up my mother and leave us kids shuddering in the dark wondering what would happen next [Alta shuddered at the very thought], but Joe doesn't do that, never has, and since I've lived with him for fifteen years he probably never will—" she broke and laughed in a sort of surprised way. "Sure would be funny if I'd been thinking of Joe all these years as my dad. Sure would be nice if I was worried about nothing."

It was nice that Alta could arrive at her conclusions for herself.

They don't all. Sometimes they believe in their own fantasies, like Bob, who said to me, "I've had to put up with this crap from my mother and my wife, and now you. I won't do it! That's all. Do you hear?"

"What crap?" (It helps them if you use their own words, especially when they are angry.)

"You know what crap."

"No, I don't know what crap. What crap?"

"You said you were tired."

"So I'm tired. I've had a long day."

"Do you think I came here to listen to *that?* All my life I've had to hold back *my* feelings because somebody was sick—my mother was always sick. I couldn't play in the house, I couldn't fight with my brothers, I couldn't watch the late show. 'Yer ma's sick, yer ma's sick.' (Chanting in a whine.)

"Then I got married. Now Cara is sick, always sick, and I have to do the same thing to my boys—

" 'Keep quiet, your mother's sick.' *I'll* tell you who's sick.

I'm sick, that's who—sick of you women and all your ailments."

(Bob believes this.)

"Tired isn't sick." (But this time a soft answer doesn't turn it off.)

"Tired—sick—what the hell does it matter—they're all the same."

"They're not the same." (I'm deliberately needling Bob. He has been seeing me quite awhile and always he has shown respect amounting to deference. I'm delighted that he has forgotten himself to the point of talking to me as I know he talks to Cara.)

"Of *course* they're the same. You women are all just alike."

(Now it is time for him to meet a new woman.)

"*I* am just like Cara, like your mother?"

"Well" (sheepishly), "you're a woman" (smiling a little).

"I am truly a woman, but I'm not a sick, complaining woman."

"Well, most of them are."

"I'm not."

"Cara and my mother are."

"That's it, isn't it? Cara and your mother."

"Yes. Cara and my mother. All right, so you're not. I don't have to live with you."

"That may be a boon to both of us."

He laughed, and the storm was over for the time being. Don't we hear that refrain often? "You're just like all the rest."

We fall heir to all the undesirable characteristics of the person we represent at the moment. On your side of the coin, you are trying to help him meet a new person—one brand new person, not any of those skulking ghosts of the past, but someone he can relate to in the now time with no remnants of other years dragging at the relationship. You are trying to be someone he has never known, and you can help him to realize who you are only if you refuse to play any of the roles he thrusts upon you. He will keep trying to force you into the other pictures, and you will keep steadily remaining in your own picture until he comes awake to the fact that you are indeed you.

You can fall heir to some good characteristics too. If you happen to do anything right and get exaggerated praise for it, you may get the idea that you really are God, and that would be a pity. In our job we're faced with the constant necessity of reminding ourselves, "There is one good—that's God."

My first week on the job I was given a clerk. She was not a civil service employee, but what they call an N.Y.C. (Neighborhood Youth Corps) student recruited from the local high school. Her experience with the profession of counseling was somewhat less than zero, and she was fascinated with everything that took place. One day after a young male patient had left the office, she looked at me with a certain awe and said admiringly, "That guy comes in sometimes when you're not around. We've had several talks—about swimming, and horses, and about school, nothing really. But you just sort of sit there and he begins to talk to you about his problems. How do you do it?"

"That's how—by just sitting there." But I admit I felt smug. There is nothing wrong with knowing your own abilities, or with being pleased at a chance compliment, but when you find yourself expecting or even hoping for these little pats on the head, let it be a flashing yellow light: you may be getting too charmed with your own charm.

On the other hand, the minister who fails to recognize the element of charisma at work in his counseling (or even other relationships) is missing many opportunities to be of help to his people. Once I had a student who just couldn't see it, even when I had pointed it out to him.

"Amy likes you."

"I like Amy."

"I mean she seems to feel an attraction to you far beyond that of a woman for her minister or even her counselor."

"Are you talking about sex?" James displayed the contempt of youth.

"Yes."

"Look, I'm twice as young as she is. I could be her son."

"You could indeed, but so could both of her husbands have been."

"That doesn't mean a thing."

"Have it your own way."

I dropped the subject, but a few days later James went to see Amy on her ward and was shown to a small side room with two beds, where the student chaplains were accustomed to visit the patients. James flopped down on one bed, expecting that Amy would decorously seat herself on the other. She didn't. Instead she leaped on him, threw both arms and both legs around him, and tried to kiss him.

"At least I kept my cool," Jim said later. "I said in a quiet voice, 'Why this, Amy?' "

"And she said, 'Why do you think?' "

"And I said, 'Why do *you* think?' "

"And Amy said, 'No, I asked you first why do you think?' We must have sounded awfully silly."

"You probably looked silly too," I commented.

"If anyone had come in, which, thank God, they didn't . . ."

The result of this little dilemma of Jim's was that he felt he could not go back to see Amy. I thought he should, but he was scared, and Amy was deeply hurt that her friend never returned.

It is for handling feelings of affection from the females in the congregation that many ministers seem least prepared.

Judd, another of my students, older but just as naïve as Jim, found himself in a similar situation. He came into the seminar room pale and shaken. He explained to his amused colleagues: "I just asked Marianne if she wanted to talk out on the grounds as we took a little walk, and she rolled her eyes up at me and said, 'That's up to you.' "

"So we started. As we left the ward there was a little ditch, and she grabbed my hand so I helped her over. She wouldn't let go my hand, and I cut the walk kind of short. When we got back she was still sort of swinging my hand, and she asked, 'Will I see you tonight?' I asked, 'Where would I see you tonight?' and she sort of grinned and said, 'That would be up to you.' "

Suddenly he broke off. "What am I going to do? The girl is a witch. I was scandalized. I never dreamed she wasn't a nice girl."

This man has been a minister for close to twenty years. The real question is not what is he going to do, but what has he *been* doing? Has he ignored the attraction his ladies have had for him? Obviously he has not responded, but suppose one of them should get aggressive like Amy?

It is very unfair to the female members to take seriously these efforts at seduction. Their real need is to be understood and loved. Some women (and men) know only one way to get understanding—through sex. If a minister feels unsure of himself, he may react by becoming frightened like James or angry like Judd. In either case the counselee is the one who suffers most. A far better thing to do in both the foregoing instances would have been to realize ahead of time that this might happen (and wherever there is a man and a woman of any age it so often does happen) and to warn the counselee in advance that counseling does not include a love relationship in the usual sense. It can be done delicately, humorously, or seriously. If it comes early enough in the relationship, it will be a helpful limitation of the relationship between minister and member, will serve to set limits to the situation and save all concerned much embarrassment and heartache.

Early on, we talked about the love that springs from gratitude. The love of your counselees is such love, no matter
how they understand it or how you interpret it. When you
take the trouble to explain to them that you have no need or
intention of seducing them or of allowing them to seduce
you, you may get a jolt to your pride to find that they respond
with vast relief. They *don't want* to relate on a love basis with
their counselor. They sometimes take this avenue of testing
you out to see if they can trust you with their unacceptable
feelings. When they find they can, the counseling has begun.

When your counselee is of the same sex, the situation is
even more delicate, but don't be scandalized. Remember that
the church itself often fosters the homosexual reaction—in
all innocence, of course. In none of these instances is your
counselee really reacting to you. He is reacting to some fantasy
of you which he carries around inside himself without even
realizing it. You can use these mistaken images to help both
male and female parishioners, if you yourself do not yield
to any panic. To say simply to a counselee, male or female,
"Perhaps you feel that you would like to seduce me, but do
not fear, that will never happen. I have no intention of seducing you, or of allowing you to seduce me," is not to be
crude. It is true you invoke a flood of hostility, but that is
fine; on the other hand, the person more often expresses a
vast sense of relief (sometimes this proves quite a blow to
the counselor's own pride!). You will find that after the
decks have been cleared by such a frank and open statement
as the above, your counselee will begin to discuss other subjects and to express feelings on a deeper level. You will remember that sex comes late in an infant's development and
to talk about sex may be easier for the person than to talk
about some more painful subjects. But if you accept his more
unacceptable sex wishes without too much excitement, he
will let you into the even less acceptable levels of his misery.
This next level is quite apt to be a hostile one.

Sometimes the charisma seems to be in reverse. That is when it is of a hostile nature. But don't worry. It makes little difference whether the feeling your counselee has for you is a negative or a positive one. If he has strong feelings about you, you can help him. Your counselee sits and bites his nails, and says nothing, or looks embarrassed, or sullen. It is a good guess he is feeling hostile toward you. He forgets to come, or comes late; he brings you gifts, or he breaks his leg! He may be feeling hostile toward you. Some of the aforementioned sexual advances may in actuality be hostile acts disguised in the garb of sex. Thus disguised, hostility becomes even more difficult to handle. But if the counselor is always on the alert for it, one finds that it can be recognized very readily. When his feelings can be dealt with before they become too strong or too threatening, the counselee learns to fear his true emotions less, and this, after all, is the real purpose of counseling.

I remember Ellis, a student from a small Midwestern seminary who came to the training center, eager and ready to work. His first criticism was of the casual schedule we followed. The other students like it, but Ellis complained about being on his own. He came every day demanding that I pick out a patient for him, and I invariably replied that he could talk to any patient on male admissions he found interesting.

"But what do you want me to *say* to them?"

"I don't care what you say to them. Just write up your conversation verbatim, and we'll discuss it. In that way I will get acquainted with both you and the patient."

"But that's not going to *help* me—or him either."

"I'll discuss your verbatim report with you and try to help you see how you can improve your technique."

"But you won't *require* anything of me."

"Then I guess you'll just have to learn to require something of yourself."

He doubled up his fist as he stood over me, and I looked steadily back at him wondering if he would hit me. He didn't. Instead he said, "This is driving me nuts," and stormed out of the room.

For three days he didn't come back. He ate with the other students, occupied his room at night, but that is all he did. For three days he played golf. At last he came back and confronted me.

"Look, I played golf three days this week."

"Have I complained about that? Have I criticized you for it?"

"No, but the summer is half over, and I'm not getting anything out of the training."

"Perhaps the greatest thing you could get out of the summer is to discover that you can cut seminars, interviews, lectures, and play golf three days, and nobody will care. For once you are completely on your own. You paid for the training—it's your time—what you choose to do with it is your business."

After that a change came over Ellis. He settled down, reappeared at seminars, picked a patient and wrote a beautiful case history on him. Furthermore, the patient's doctor told me the patient had shown a marked improvement as a result of his talks with Ellis.

But the greatest change was in his talks with me. He stopped being critical of me and began criticizing another chaplain on the staff. He would fly into a purple rage at the memory of some of the chaplain's rigid ways. At last one morning Ellis began to talk of his father—a man rigid like the chaplain and full of self-righteous anger, unbending in his demands on his family, always requiring perfection of Ellis, who was the oldest child.

One day I suggested he might like to tear up a copy of the church magazine—published by his father's church. He responded with gusto and tore it across and across again until he had it in several hunks. Then he stood up and flung each separate hunk down on the floor with all his strength.

Then he sat down, put his head in his hands, and his big frame trembled. Finally he rose with a thin smile, scooped up the scattered paper, balled it up, and, with nothing like the energy he had used earlier, threw it in the wastebasket.

"Thanks," he grinned as he left.

During all this time I had said not a word.

The best way to attack this entrenched misery is to sit and listen—to listen and listen. When I suggest that a counselor sit and listen to a counselee for thirty to forty-five minutes in dead silence, I am usually met with vigorous resistance, for silence, though golden, is most uncomfortable to many of us. We have learned to "make conversation." To unlearn this parlor trick and assume a virtue of sympathetic silence is a most difficult task. I do not think that the counselee will suffer from knowing your opinions, or from helpful comments or questions, but I do think that the necessity for learning silence will make it imperative that you first listen and then, as you gradually develop your own method with people, begin to make a few comments.

Comments that do not threaten or hurt a counselee usually contain some quotation from himself. A person can bear his own statement even when it is paraphrased for the use of the counselor. But to say, for instance, "That bothers you, doesn't it?" is not to break the train of the patient's thought. To comment, "I wonder why you blush when you make that statement," or to suggest, "It seems that you are a bit uncomfortable when mentioned that." All these things encourage the counselee to talk about various parts of his personality which you may have sensed were giving him trouble, without, at the same time, ramming your own opinions down his throat or bringing into a threatening glare of light some painful subject that he prefers to cover with shadows. Many

175

times the shadows are for his own use, and the real truth is obvious to everyone but himself. To treat gently these spots of pain in the beginning will prove quite rewarding in the end. The counselee needs, in the first few sessions, to learn that he can say anything to you without being hurt or frightened, and since you realize the dangers that threaten him from the demons that possess his soul, you will be more tolerant and able to listen as he continues his journey into the world of the past. Many things that he will say may ring strangely in your ears, but remember that you are here not to avoid unpleasant subjects, that silence is golden, that hostility is healing, that pain marks the growing edge of personality, that delinquent and defiant behavior often represents certain stages of the growth of the personality, that one's counselee may get worse before he gets better.

So you sit in one chair, and your counselee sits in the other. What will you be today? His father, his mother? Who can tell? But if you can accept with equanimity and unconditional love all and anything that this man may have to say, it is certain that throughout the relationship you will be his friend. In the end we trust that he will drop the false ideas he has held about you, that you will no longer be one of the figures that terrorized and betrayed him in his childhood, but that he will see you as you are with all your faults and learn that he can love you as you are without fear or undue admiration; that he can accept himself as a man and an equal, who is neither better nor worse than you and all men; and that he can relax in the confidence that he is accepted in like manner.

To develop in him this attitude of mind and heart you, too, must have a realistic view of yourself and him. At no time can you enter with him into the fantasy that there is something godlike about *you!* To be a person and not just a minister is your object as you relate to this individual who so desperately needs you. At this point he does not need the ancient magic of the medicine man; he needs a human being who can meet him and talk to him as one man to another without fear and without pride. It was such an attitude in Jesus that made men leave their nets to follow him.

11

The Truth Shall Make You Free

"Oh, there you are, you wonderful woman of God! Come over here. I want to talk to you."

I went.

Sally was a cute little brunette patient I had seen a few times. She had been in the hospital two weeks, and already she was showing signs of improvement. She spoke rapidly in a rather high-pitched, artificial voice—like a train whistle off-key.

"I had a vision. Do you believe in visions?"

Without waiting for a reply she continued.

"The Holy Ghost visited me. I had been having a lot of trouble with my husband, and all this financial difficulty, and I was sloppy and fat and didn't take care of myself." (She dropped back to a normal tone.) "Look at me now. I have

178

slimmed down. I'm wearing nail polish and lipstick. I'm even going to the entertainment tonight."

"That's nice."

"So I was having all this trouble with my husband, [resuming her train-whistle voice], and I was fasting. I hadn't had anything but prayed-over water for ten days. One night I was lying in my bed, and the Holy Ghost visited me there. He was the most beautiful man. His face was milk-white and clear. You could not distinguish his features. They were just a white blur, but his arms were pure gold (she gestured, running her hands up and down her own arms), and he carried a lamp that high (raising her hand about six feet off the floor) filled with shining multi-colored jewels and covered with gold filigree, and then the Holy Ghost passed over me and he filled me with a white substance."

All this had been blurted out like one sentence without pausing for breath. Again she dropped her train whistle.

" 'Twasn't milk," she confided, her eyes twinkling with genuine humor.

"I wonder what all that meant to you." (Ignoring the joke.)

"I thought that Armageddon was coming for the world, but I was wrong. *The real Armageddon was coming in my spirit.* Do you know what I mean?"

"Well, I think so, but tell me anyway."

"Now that I am better, I think the vision was personal rather than cosmic."

"You express yourself well."

"I've got a lot of degrees. Do you think I'm crazy?"

"Do *you* think you are?"

"Sometimes." (Again that touch of humor with the knowing smile.)

Can a production so "crazy" have any meaning? Can it be religious in any sense of the word? Can it teach us any-

thing about her, her parents, or her relationship to them?
Let's see.

The next day Sally showed me a letter from her mother.
It was filled with the smallest kind of small talk, illustrated
with stick drawings like a homemade comic strip. It would
have been appropriate for a kindergartner, but certainly not
for a university graduate.

"I don't like this. She makes me so mad. I wish I could
tell her so."

"You can. There's the phone."

I heard only Sally's end of the conversation, but I had to
smile at the contrast between her announced anger, which
had been the occasion for the call, and the actual tone with
which she addressed her mother.

"Hello—hello—oh, hello, Mother. How are you? . . . I'm
fine. I'm getting better all the time. . . . They treat me very
well here. . . . Yes, I have plenty to eat. . . . Mother, I'm
with the chaplain—a lady—isn't that something? . . . I'm
going to the entertainment tonight. . . . Oh, Jack's sister is
taking care of the child. [She always referred to her little
daughter as "it" or "the child."] . . .

"Now, Mother, don't work too hard. . . . I wish I could see
you, too. . . . Good-bye. I love you."

She turned away from the phone, her eyes glistening with
tears.

"Do you feel better?"

"Oh, yes!"

I didn't remind her that she'd phoned to express anger.
Sally felt better, so we carried on from there.

"My mother is so good, and I have given her so much
trouble."

"You have?"

"Yes. She says I tore her unmercifully. I wish I could
make it up to her."

"*Tore* her?"

"Yes, when I was born."

"Sally, you have a daughter, don't you?"

"Yes, eight years old."

"Do you blame her for *your* labor pains?"

"Well, I didn't have any trouble with Ruth."

"Ruth? Isn't that your mother's name?"

"Yes, it's my baby's name too. She is named for Mother." (Now I know why you call her "it" or "the child.")

"Well, do you blame her—*could* you blame her—even if you'd had a hard labor?"

"I didn't."

"Sally, was she to blame for your labor pains? She caused them, yes, in a certain sense—but can you *blame* her?"

"Of course not."

"Then why do you blame yourself for your mother's labor pains."

"Hey!" (Delighted.) "That's one way of looking at it, isn't it?"

Sally laughed and sobered immediately. "But Mother blames me."

And she did too. One day Sally's mother described in great detail the labor pains she had suffered when Sally was born. "Sally tore me unmercifully," she said to me in such a way I was sure it must be something her mother said often.

"How long ago was that?"

"Well" (irritably), "Sally's thirty-one."

"Isn't that a pretty long time to be holding it against her? Do you think she did it deliberately?"

"Of course not, but you can't forget a thing like that."

"Can you forgive it?"

"*Miss* Long, I wonder they let you work here—you are so unfeeling. You have no kindness. I'm sorry I ever tried to talk to you about Sally!"

"Have you been talking about Sally?"

"Of course—if you want to be *that way* . . ."

So I learned about Sally's mother. Sally's father had been stabbed to death by an irate neighbor on Sally's eighth birthday. Soon afterward Sally began having nightmares and wetting the bed. Her grades at school dropped to F. Her behavior in class became disruptive. The school psychologist suggested that she be put in a nearby institution for disturbed children.

After three years Sally seemed better. Her mother had remarried. Sally returned home, but all was not for the best. Sally was eleven by now. Her little friends weren't quite so little anymore. The new stepfather would embarrass her by hanging around and by fondling the little girls Sally brought home from school. After a bit, none of her friends would accept Sally's invitation to go home after school.

But Sally was growing older every day, and soon the gap in her social life was being filled with boys—mostly older boys. At sixteen Sally fell in love with Melvin, a G.I. She believed Melvin when he said he wanted to marry her, and her wedding plans were almost completed when he went off to Korea without a word to Sally. By now she was eighteen and in college. She buried herself in her books and graduated *cum laude* in three years with summer school. She got her M.A. degree the next year and seemed to be doing very well when Melvin returned, married to a WAC.

Sally had been sporadically dating a man who was eighteen years older than she. She married him, and the next year Ruth was born. Her course had been downward from then on, but her real break with reality came on Ruth's eighth birthday (on her own eighth birthday, remember, her father had been killed).

Sally was already getting better when I started counseling her, and she improved steadily. At first she used to talk a great deal about the Holy Ghost who had visited her, but one day I noticed that she was now calling him an angel, which I took to be a mark of improvement. (Is it any less crazy to be visited by an angel than by the Holy Ghost? I thought so.) Soon she stopped talking about the vision altogether and began to have a good deal to say about her Father in heaven. At first I wasn't sure whether she meant God or her dead father, but I soon found out. She meant both, and she had them confused in her mind.

It was another month before she separated them, but all the time she was telling me more and more about her feelings about things in the real world. She told me all about the stabbing. She spoke of her father in a most idealistic way at first, but finally she began to say just a few things about him that painted him as all too human—like, "I was only a little girl, but I remember too well the strap that hung behind the cellar door, and how he used to tell me after he beat me with it that one day he would throw me down those dark cellar stairs. He never did, but one of the first things I thought of after he was killed was that I needn't worry any more about him throwing me down those dark stairs. Then I felt horrid for thinking it."

She said a few things about her mother, such as "Mother's last husband used to beat her, but I guess she asked for it." Or, "When Mother came to see me and Jack in New York she tried to change my apartment all around to suit herself. Jack just told her one day it was my apartment and I could decorate it any way I liked. Mother left in a fit of rage, and she hasn't liked Jack since."

Finally she made a few feeble attempts to express some of her enormous rage at me, but in a very gentle and roundabout way: "You are a wonderful woman and I like to talk to you, but even though I am a Protestant, I have to go to Catholic services on Sunday. I see enough women. I have to go see Father Matthew, that wonderful man of God. Isn't he just the most beautiful thing you ever saw?" And without waiting for a reply, "I am on the ward with women patients, the technicians are all women, the doctor is a woman, and you are a woman. I have to look at a man sometimes."

"Of course you do."

She seemed a little startled that I took it so mildly. Next week she tried again:

"Please do not speak to me now, Ma'am. I am walking with my work detail, and I cannot stop." (I'd only said "Hello" in passing.) Or "I have a great deal of respect for you, Ma'am."

"Why do you call me 'Ma'am' sometimes?"

"Well, that's what you are, isn't it?" And she repeated, "I have a great deal of respect for you."

I said, "Yes, but you use that respect to build a barrier around yourself because you are afraid of having any closer friendship with me. Isn't that true?"

It was soon after this that her mother was planning to call again. This time she said, "My mother is going to call me, and I dread it. She will ask me all about how I am getting along with Jack, and I shudder to think what all she will pry out of me."

"If my own conversation with your mother is a fair sample, all you have to do is ask *her* a question and stand there until she slows down, then ask her another question."

She laughed merrily, delighted at so frank an appraisal of her hitherto untouchable mother.

The next time I saw her, she confessed that she was terrified of God and thought he would punish her horribly for her sins, a quite different attitude from the chummy one she had assumed at first. Finally she began to accept God as having a few pure motives, and for the first time she began to trust him.

"I think I had God my Father in Heaven confused with my dead father in Heaven, and some things I really hated in my father when he was alive I attributed to God the Father because I was afraid to think bad thoughts about Daddy. I must have been terrorized by him as a child—it makes me feel sorry for the child that was me."

Many things can be learned from Sally. The most obvious, of course, is the symbolic condensation of her need for a good husband and her deeper need for a good father in her "vision"—which she described as a sexual experience with the "Holy Ghost." In every act her hunger for a father is obvious: in her going to the Catholic services because I was a woman; in her need to express her hostile feelings toward her mother (me); in her marrying a man eighteen years older than she was; in her fears and longings toward her father in Heaven, by which she showed that her neurotic religious manifestations were tightly bound to her very practical and earthly needs. I accepted more and more of her forgotten wishes that were not acceptable to her, as they had not been to her own mother, and she took me more and more into her confidence. As often as I could, I acted as I was sure her mother would never act, and in this way alleviated some of her fears of persons in authority. What made Sally ill? Her mother blamed Sally's mother-in-law. Jack blamed the experience of her father's being stabbed to death. The staff of the hospital said Sally was "off" on the subject of religion. Personally, I think that her troubles began much earlier. Her mother did not really want a baby when Sally arrived. Both mother and father were excessively severe with Sally as a small child. The death of her father and the subsequent training she had in Sunday school gave her a cloak for her emotional disturbance, but she was not "off" on the subject of religion. At times it becomes necessary to disregard the form and examine the content of her religious visions and ideas.

Many counselors take the attitude that a man's religion is sacred and not to be monkeyed with. Your counselee, quick to fend off every hurt and every self-revelation that might lead to a hurt, will hide behind his religion as often as he feels he can get by with doing so. Herein lies both our privilege and our obligation. As ministers we dare not enter into the superstitious attitude that a man's religion, however sick and warped, is sacred just because it is called by the name of religion. On the contrary, we, of all people, can divide the wheat of true religion from the chaff of neurosis in the people who seek our help.

What does the counselee mean? He *says* he sees the devil or has lost faith, or has changed his faith, or has a vision of God in some form or other, but what does he *mean?* Look for the answer at home. Remember the succinct words of Jesus, "Go and fetch your husband." Religion that is not neurotic is comforting, not disturbing. If a church member comes to you with a problem about religion, look again. He has chosen a subject that is taboo to keep you from probing into painful material, but in his deepest heart he *wants* you to disregard the taboo and exorcise the demons that live inside him. Look first for the guilt, then for the hostility that produces the guilt. Too often ministers seek to arouse guilt by moralizing or giving advice and then become angry if the counselee does not follow their authoritarian dictates.

Jesus practiced the art of relieving guilt: "Let not your heart be troubled."

"I came to seek and to save the lost."

"The well have no need of a physician."

We can all arouse feelings of guilt—for, like Sally's, the guilt is already there just waiting to be activated. It takes an artist to alleviate guilt, to destroy the neurotic guilt, to treat with gentleness and understanding the justified guilt. The ability to relieve guilt is an art that springs from a lively confidence in the inner and basic goodness, in God's understanding, and in one's own self as a counselor. Only with such a faith can a counselor sit in silence, withholding both judgment and premature reassurance, as the counselee struggles.

Never fear—he will say everything we, ourselves, can

allow ourselves to hear. All of us are alike in our deepest selves: much worse and at the same time much better than we like to admit. Do not fear either that you will "destroy his faith" if you turn the searchlight of truth on it. Long ago the writer of Hebrews gave us a guideline for that:

> Now he [God] hath promised, saying, "Yet once more I shake not the earth only, but also heaven." And this word, "Yet once more," signifieth the removing of those things that are shaken . . . that those things which cannot be shaken may remain. Wherefore we [now receive] a kingdom which cannot be moved."

So at last it is Sunday morning, and you mount the pulpit, engulfed in a crescendo of organ music. You look out over the congregation, and they look back. Through the week you are their counselor and friend, you play golf with them, you bury their dead and marry their willing, you are a man among them, subject to the sins and angers and loves that they are subject to—and through it all you try to demonstrate the unconditional love of God. But today a new dimension has been added—at once historic and prophetic, a dimension that clothes you in the garments of poetic fantasy. Some of you will wear the robes that enhance this unique role, some will scorn any such fancy dress, but all will wear the garment of the holy. In and out among the Gothic arches dances the shadow, cast by flickering candlelight, of the medicine man—your shadow.

You take a covert look at your congregation. There they sit, a group of twentieth-century moderns—perfumed, be-furred, sophisticated. All look toward you and the altar with expectation in their faces. You know them all so well, and as your glance passes among them you remember little things they've said. Mentally you take a reading:

The Drakes sit in a prim line together halfway back. "We

come to church because it is our Christian duty. We are obligated." (They have a long way to go.)

The Macs are scattered out in an uneven line of humanity across the front row. "We think religion gives you a lift. We work in the church because we're grateful, not because we're scared." (You could use a few more like that.)

Julia and Arnie are near the back tenderly sharing a basket of squirming human flesh. "We never felt so close to God as when the twins were born." (This is Julia's first time back in church since they arrived.)

Big Jim sits proud and tall beside his married daughter Tina and her husband; his wife sits on the other side of him with the younger children. "I've been chairman of every board in this church, but I never knew before how the love of God really feels."

You catch a glimpse of Mel and Maggie in the balcony. "If this is religion, we want it."

Here comes old Stoney—for weeks now he's been staying away just to show you—and look who else! His whole family moves into the pew they usually occupy. Last to come in is Janice and, after her, Stan. He surreptitiously flashes you a peace sign as he takes his place among the family. (You never thought you'd see him there!)

Stoney sits there staring at you as if his very life depended on you, as indeed it does. He is your newest and shyest counselee. He is wondering if you will inadvertently betray some confidence he has divulged during the week. He hopes that you will somehow speak to the need that boils within him. He has been staying away because he wants to let you know how little he depends on you. But this has been a good week for him. Whether he comes for relief and comfort or stays away to express his fear and anger, he expects more of you than any man can give. He is not able to put into words the unreasoning faith he has in you. He does not even know why he has such confidence in your ability. Yet through some alchemy his spirit recognizes in you the prehistoric medicine man, and he knows that you, and only you, can chase away the evil spirits that plague him. Partly he expects what he would expect of any psychologist, doctor, or social worker he might have chosen as his counselor, but he expects more than he would from any one of them, because of the special relationship you are supposed to have with the Almighty. On a deeper level entirely unknown to him, in the realm of forgotten feelings, he is expecting you to become again that ancient purveyor of magic, who, by incantations and gestures and the ritualistic doing and undoing of the church service, will exorcise the demons that torment his soul.

All of them look to you as men have looked at their priest for thousands of years. Much of the ritual of your church service—the chants, the songs, the offering, the sacramental acts—will speak to needs as deep as life itself, as long as history, as high as heaven. The most primitive needs of your people will be met, and their unreasoning fears relieved by the acts that you and they will perform during this service. You pray that God will take away the hearts of stone and give them hearts that can be touched.

Now the music has ceased, the offering is on the altar, a hush of expectation rises toward you like a wave. You ascend the pulpit, you open the book, and you begin your sermon:

"You shall know the truth, and the truth shall make you free."